Change in Organisations

DEDICATION

Dedicated to all who have participated with me
in learning about organisational life

Change in Organisations

Petrūska Clarkson

Whurr Publishers Ltd
London

© 1995 Petrūska Clarkson
Whurr Publishers Ltd
19b Compton Terrace, London N1 2UN, England

Reprinted 1997

All rights reserved. No part of this publication may be reproduced, stored in a retrieval system, or transmitted in any form of by any means, electronic, mechanical, photocopying, recording or otherwise, without the prior permission of Whurr Publishers Limited.

This publication is sold subject to the condition that it shall not, by way of trade or otherwise, be lent, resold, hired out, or otherwise circulated without the publisher's prior consent in any form of binding or cover other than that in which it is published and without a similar condition including this condition being imposed upon any subsequent purchaser.

British Library Cataloguing in Publication Data
A catalogue record for his book is available from the British Library.

ISBN 1-897635-33-8

Printed and bound in the UK by Athenaeum Press Ltd,
Gateshead, Tyne & Wear

Contents

Preface	vii
Contributors	x
Outline of the book	xi
Acknowledgements	xv

Chapter 1

Core competencies in organisational consulting	1
   Petrūska Clarkson

Chapter 2

The scope of stress counselling at work	7
   Petrūska Clarkson

Chapter 3

Redundancy counselling	15
   Petrūska Clarkson

Chapter 4

The differential outcomes of organisational change	26
   Petrūska Clarkson

Chapter 5

Prioritising organisational interventions – a diagnostic	34
framework: what goes wrong in management
consultancy, and some pointers how to minimise it
   Petrūska Clarkson and *Kamil Kellner*

Chapter 6

Human relationships at work in organisations	43
   Petrūska Clarkson and *Patricia Shaw*

Chapter 7

Professional development, personal development and counselling and psychotherapy: how to differentiate and negotiate boundaries in organisational work 56
Petrūska Clarkson and *Susan Clayton*

Chapter 8

The pseudocompetent executive: Achilles at work 76
Petrūska Clarkson

Chapter 9

Stages of group development and the group imago: a comparative analysis of the stages of the group process 85
Petrūska Clarkson

Chapter 10

A small kitbag for the future: survival skills for the next century 107
Petrūska Clarkson

Chapter 11

Bystanding in organisations: A block to empowerment 121
Petrūska Clarkson and *Patrica Shaw*

Chapter 12

2500 years of gestalt: From Heraclitus to the big bang 126
Petrūska Clarkson

Chapter 13

Burn-out: Unhelpful personality patterns of professional helpers 140
Petrūska Clarkson

Index 149

Preface

This book consists of a selection of papers written by me alone and with colleagues. Some have been previously published, and others have been specifically written for this book to show 'psychology at work'.

Organisations will be introduced as a complex web of human relationships – an original framework for differentiating different facets of such relationships. These are

- the *working alliance*
- the *unfinished* or *projected* relationship
- the *developmental* relationship
- the *personal* relationship
- the *transpersonal* relationship.

The idea of any organisation as a field system of interacting relationships is central to my work, and I will draw on insights emerging from sociocultural influences, physics, psychology and philosophy to provide fertile metaphors that lead to practical implications for the effective functioning of organisations in the postmodern world.

The relationship skills and competencies covered are many of those needed to create the kind of healthy and productive interaction between people at work which sustains the capacity to make organisational wholes. We will use this as a basis for distinguishing the potential contribution of leaders, managers and specialists working as members of an organisation, as well as the various external consulting and psychological counselling services available.

This book will seek to provide readers with a satisfying sampling of the experience of working within or with organisations, sound conceptual frameworks for understanding that experience and practical help in transforming its possibilities. I would encourage readers to choose which chapters to read first: some will be of more interest than others. For example, Chapter 3 will probably be useful mainly to people with an interest in gestalt as well as outplacement counselling. On the other hand, most people find Chapter 10 useful.

Who Is This Book For?

The book could be of interest to a number of different groups.

- Clinical, occupational and counselling psychologists who want to extend their ability to work with organisational systems in addition to individuals and groups.
- Organisational consultants and organisational development practitioners, both internal and external, for whom this book will provide a perspective on intervention in organisations.
- Trainers and management development specialists who will find in the book a comprehensive framework for assessing and developing human relationship competencies vital to organisations.
- Students at management colleges, universities and business schools for whom this will provide an original contribution to organisational theory, well grounded in the literature and fully referenced.
- Practising leaders, managers and specialists with a thirst for some help in thinking about and engaging effectively with their organisations as human systems.

Why Is It Needed?

Since the 1930s work in organisations has involved firstly the appreciation of the limits of mechanistic perspective and then the development of the human relations school, whose psychological base was primarily psychoanalytic. In the 1960s, organisations flirted incautiously with the different humanistic therapeutic approaches mushrooming everywhere, and to some extent withdrew with burnt fingers. Although many of the major textbooks on organisational behaviour, organisational psychology and management development recognise and repeatedly refer to the need for 'people skills' and interpersonal effectiveness, there is a lack of coherent and substantial formulations which draw on all our available sources of psychological and social understanding. It is perhaps time for a re-assessment and a fresh integration of the knowledge gained, which is in line with the paradigm emerging in many fields of scientific as well as philosophic enquiry.

This is particularly important when organisations are struggling to learn how to function effectively in an increasingly turbulent, less clearly structured world. It is our belief and experience that *relationship* is a key concept for our times, which can provide underlying order and meaning in chaotic conditions. Recent popular organisational texts such as *When Giants Learn to Dance* (Kanter), *Thriving on Chaos* (Peters), *Riding the Waves of Change* (Morgan) and *The Age of Unreason* (Handy) describe and explore the implications for organisations in the late twentieth century environment. Organisational counselling psychology is also currently emerging as a discipline in its own right (see L.H. Gerstein and S.L. Shullman, in *Handbook of Counselling Psychology*, ed. S.D. Brown and R.W. Lent, New York: Wiley, 1992). Of course all professionals – particularly counsellors, psychologists, psychoanalysts and psychotherapists of all persuasions – inextricably work within an organisational context, even if it is their own professional body, and in addition most if not all their clients live and work in organisations.

In writing the book I have been able to draw on almost 30 years of work in the field of human relationships and organisation development. My original academic perspective has been well honed in the real world of clinical and counselling psychology practice, freelance organisational consultancy and the leadership and management of organisations. I am also fortunate that as a consultant I can draw from my enormously valuable experience as the author and originator of the **metanoia** training institute for psychotherapists and counsellors. In April 1994 I had the satisfaction of accomplishing the positioning of the vision and organisation which I had built, managed and led for over two decades from obscurity to international eminence, in a trust managed by individuals who had both shaped and been shaped by the organisation for many years.

Primarily my background covers psychology and philosophy, while my work experience has been in an additional wide variety of settings – group and individual psychotherapy practice, counselling, training and supervision of counsellors, clinical and occupational psychologists, psychotherapists and consultants, organisational training, organisational consulting in local government, the public sector and multinational companies. I now work independently under the name of Physis in London and abroad. I love solving problems.

Contributors

Petrüska Clarkson, PhD, is a Consultant Chartered Clinical and Counselling Psychologist, counsellor, mentor, psychotherapist, and supervisor. She has been an independent organisation development consultant in public and private sectors for more than two decades. She has designed or co-designed several national and internationally accredited courses on these subjects and is founder or has been chair/training and supervisor of many organisations in these fields. She now works internationally and independently under the name of Physis, is a visiting lecturer at several universities in Britain and abroad and has published more than eighty professional papers and eight books in these fields.

Susan Clayton is a Chartered Psychologist and practising organisational consultant, facilitator and mentor. She is the managing director of **feedback** change consultancy limited and is a leading contributor to the development and practice of Gestalt in organisations. She is a graduate of the Organisational Consultancy Diploma programme led by Dr Clarkson.

Kamil Kellner, MSc, Fellow of Institute of Personnel and Development, Member of Association for Management Education and Development, teaches consulting and organisational development at South Bank Business School, works as an organisational consultant, consults to and trains practising consultants.

Patricia Shaw is an Independent Organisational Consultant currently on the Doctoral programme at Hertford Business School with Professor Stacey. She is a graduate of the Organisational Consultancy Diploma programme led by Dr Clarkson.

Outline of the book

Chapter 1 – Core competencies in organisational consulting – outlines in brief form the six major areas of organisational core competencies and three primary aspects of each. This forms a core syllabus around which any consultant, novice or experienced, can organise their own training, development and further education. The six areas cover

- contracting
- connection
- comprehension
- conduct
- cautions
- credit (or evaluation).

Chapter 2 – The scope of stress counselling at work – provides a broad perspective on the scope of counselling in organisations conceptualised around *stress*. Two intersecting dimensions are postulated – that of the *individual* and the *organisation*, and that of *distress* and *eustress.* By means of a discussion of the quadrants thus created, the provision of counselling services, training and consultancy can be conceptualised, re-evaluated and broadened to include, not only prevention and limitation of the effects of negatively experienced stress, but also the cultivation and enhancement of positively experienced stress (eustress).

Chapter 3 – Redundancy counselling – introduces the cyclic nature of all experience as it is understood in gestalt terms. In our work training people in counselling skills to help individuals deal with being made redundant, we have found it useful to use the idea of a *cycle of human experience*. This helps trainees understand the different phases and reactions of individuals to major life events such as redundancy, and also to locate different counselling skills at different points on the cycle.

Chapter 4 – The differential outcomes of organisational change – concerns the assessment of the effects of organisational consultancy, restructuring or an organisational development intervention including some of the dangers. It explores potential outcomes of change in terms of five kinds of change – real change, making progress, disillusionment, disintegration and false change – the illusion of autonomy. It is a tool both for diagnosis, planning and also particularly for evaluating.

Chapter 5 – Prioritising organisational interventions – a diagnostic framework is subtitled 'What Goes Wrong in Management Consultancy, and Some Pointers to how to Minimise it" A framework is developed as a diagnostic tool to help novice and experienced consultants, trainers and supervisors establish clarity and criteria for deciding

- what is most important in a specific situation
- how to select what to do next
- which factors to give most urgent attention.

It uses the categories of *danger, confusion, conflict* and *deficit* as aid to think through and act effectively in the organisational context.

Chapter 6 – Human relationships at work in organisations – discusses an organisation as a collection of people who generate between and around them a network of relationships. We distinguish five different strands of relationship at work and consider both their contribution to productive and satisfying organisational life and their potential for creating problems. We also look at the range of counselling and consulting skills and services which can support the healthy functioning of this network of relationships.

Chapter 7 – Professional development, personal development and counselling and psychotherapy – subtitled 'How to Differentiate and Negotiate Boundaries in Organisational Work', is largely about understanding and setting boundaries. It covers

- doing (professional development)
- being (counselling and psychotherapy)
- personal development
- the differences and boundaries between them as well as leadership and facilitation skills in boundary management.

Chapter 8 – The pseudocompetent executive: Achilles at work – summarises some of my work on the Achilles syndrome – the mismatch between competence and confidence which lead to people feeling like a fraud, over-stressed and underachieving. It covers the nature of the learning cycle in organisational life as well as ways of diagnosing when where and how to re-establish the natural human desire to learn as well as to unlearn old and unproductive habits.

Chapter 9 – Stages of group development and the group imago – is a comparative analysis of the stages of the group process. This chapter compares Berne's concepts of group imago adjustment with the stages of group development as conceptualized by Tuckman (1965) and Lacoursiere (1980). It utilises Bernean diagrams of group dynamics in order to explain the nature of the processes involved at different stages in the maturation of a group. It also considers some of the most relevant tasks of group leaders at the different stages whetherthe group leaders be trainers, organisational consultants or group psychotherapists. Finally, it summarizes the most relevant constructive and destructive group leader behaviours at different phases.

Chapter 10 – A small kitbag for the future: survival skills for the next century – reveals how many professionals in the area of management and organisational development now reluctantly but sincerely realise that we no longer know for sure what to teach or how to help those who are struggling to be effective in the turbulent organisations of today. Nevertheless, the need for help and the desire to help remain. This chapter is one such attempt to collect a kitbag of useful management tools for the future. It identifies some metaphors for understanding, necessary skills, useful attitudes and facilitative behaviours for current and future conditions.

Chapter 11 – Bystanding in organisations – briefly summarises some of the examples and types of *bystanding* which occur in organisations when individuals feel disempowered to take responsibility in situations of injustice, cruelty or bad business ethics.

Chapter 12 – 2500 Years of Gestalt, from Heraclitus to the big bang – It is suggested in this chapter that there are three themes which, although they overlap and interact themselves as wholes, between them embrace the most important emphases in gestalt. These are:

- everything is a whole
- everything changes
- everything is related to everything else.

These themes are traced from their earliest source in the western tradition – Heraclitus – through Smuts and Perls to the constantly changing frontiers of scientific enquiry, such as quantum physics and chaos theory. It is suggested that these sources (the most ancient and the most modern) are to be counted, acknowledged and used as theoretical works in the gestalt canon with great implication for conceptualisation, method, attitude and technique. These applications may be to individual or organisational work.

Chapter 13 – Burn-out: Unhelpful personality pattens of professional helpers – reviews the tendency to burn-out (the depletion of energy levels) of those in the caring professions. There is a relationship among scripts, life positions, and Freudenberger's personality types. This relationship is represented by three distinct racket systems, which are relevant to various predispositions to burn-out in the helping professions. These three typologies, with their associated fairy story characters, are offered as a guide to enhancing understanding for differing personality types' experience of burn-out, rather than as a characterisation of individuals.

Overall, these papers are a selection of a much larger body of resources which has proved helpful to students, colleagues and organisations over the last couple of decades. They can be roughly related to the core competency areas covered in the eponymous chapter. Their range, style and application is quite varied and individual. This reflects their history. Please read only those which appeal to you, and in any order.

Each one was originally developed as a response to particular problems in the practice of management and consultancy or training and supervision of psychologists and other organisational consultants. Each one was born from a problem for which the existing paradigms were not sufficient, useful or welcome. This combination reflects something of my consultancy style – to enter each assignment anew and find or make the theory and discover or develop skills which are most likely to enable that organisation to achieve its optimum functioning, in its own idiom, idiosyncratic style and particularly favoured ways of thinking and doing.

In order to contextualise it congruently in this way, each chapter starts with a fictionalised scene or problem set by the parameters of the consultancy assignment, and ends with references or suggested futher reading.

Acknowledgements

I am grateful to the editors of the following books and journals for publication of material which forms portions of this book:

Chapter 2 is based on 'The Scope of Stress Counselling in Organisations' by P. Clarkson, which was published in 1990 by *Employee Counselling Today*, 2(4), pp. 3–6.

Chapter 6 is based on 'Human Relationships at Work – The Place of Counselling Skills and Consulting Skills and Services in Organisations' by P. Clarkson and P. Shaw, which was published in 1992 by *MEAD, the Journal of the Association of Management Education and Development*, 23(1), pp. 18–29.

Chapter 8 is based on 'Achilles at Work: The Pseudocompetent Executive' by P. Clarkson, which was published in 1994 in *The Achilles Syndrome: Overcoming the Secret Fear of Failure*, pp. 63–73. Shaftesbury, Dorset: Element.

Chapter 9 is based on 'Group Imago and the Stages of Group Development: A Comparative Analysis of the Stages of the Group Process' by P. Clarkson, which was published in 1988 by *ITA News*, 20, pp. 4–16. (An abbreviated version of the paper appeared in *Group Relations* (1991), pp. 14–17.)

Chapter 10 is based on 'A Small Kitbag for the Future' by P. Clarkson, which was published in *Order, Chaos and Change in the Public Sector: Papers from the Third Public Sector Conference organised by AMED*, 18–20 January 1993, pp. 17–27.

Chapter 12 is based on '2,500 years of Gestalt – From Heraclitus to the Big Bang' by P. Clarkson, which was published in 1993 by *British Gestalt Journal*, 2(1), pp. 4–9.

Chapter 13 is based on 'Burnout' by P. Clarkson, which was published in 1988 by *ITA News*, 9, pp. 4–8. (Versions subsequently appeared in *Transactional Analysis Journal*, 22 (3), pp. 153–158, and in P. Clarkson (1992) *Transactional Analysis Psychotherapy: An Integrated Approach*, in the chapter on 'The Psychotherapist in Training, Supervision and

Work', pp. 257–292.

Every effort has been made to obtain permission to reproduce copyright material throughout this book. If any proper acknowledgement has not yet been made, the copyright holder should contact the publisher.

Chapter 1
Core competencies in organisational consulting

PETRŪSKA CLARKSON

The Problem

On the training and shadow consultancy programme which I lead for organisational consultants, several people had been exercising their minds on the issue of competencies in this field. The group consists of occupational and counselling psychologists, psychotherapists and counsellors as well as educational and IT specialists and professionals with Master degrees in Business Administration. They work in a variety of settings from highly commercial multinationals to sex education for adults with special needs and physical handicaps.

There had been specific requests for trainings focused on core competencies in organisational consultancy and the development of a specific syllabus to cover these. The group did not find many of the usual textbooks covering a basic review of competencies and their associated elements particularly useful. This paper was my response to the problem of categorising, labelling and sorting organisational competencies, achieved, desired and to be developed. It was designed to delineate the field and facilitate the development of a checklist of transdisciplinary competencies drawing broadly on the relevant disciplines involved.

Introduction

Organisational consulting is a hybrid profession which has grown in popularity and acceptability in the last 70 years or so. I call it a hybrid because it so often acts as an umbrella term for professionals from a wide variety of backgrounds who in one way or another act as facilitators, enablers, advisers, change agents or catalysts for organisations. The most usual primary areas which lead to organisational consulting are

- *expertise* in areas such as IT, accountancy and business engineering in the one circle
- *counselling psychology/personnel/human resources* in the second,
- *organisational psychology* including group dynamics, motivation and systemic learning in the third.

It can be envisaged as an overlapping Venn diagram.

The task of the consultant is also to be differentiated from that of trainer, manager or supervisor. Each of these has particular functions which overlap in the discipline of consultancy. These can be signposted as education, organisational responsibility, and increasing the value of the service or product.

There are primarily two kinds of consultant. One is the consultant as expert – expert in IT, financial management, corporate structure, or law. The other kind of consultant draws expertise mainly from the fields of the structure and dynamics of organisations, human motivation and communication processes, and an expertise which draws primarily from the conceptual cluster surrounding the idea of change agent, enabler, facilitator, process consultant, and so forth.

The first kind of consultant's work is primarily, though not exclusively, targeted towards its content or specific, specialised knowledge. The second kind of consultant's work is mainly concerned with process – that is, the often unmeasurable subtleties of climate, culture, atmosphere, morale, efficiency in decision making, optimal creativity and flexible resourcefulness in periods of crisis and stasis.

The core competencies can be divided into six areas:

- contract (selling)
- connection (relating)
- comprehension (understanding)
- conduct (acting)
- caution (non-acting)
- credit (learning and evaluation).

For each of these phases there are many competencies which are probably essential to the effective and efficient accomplishment of the task of consultancy. We will identify some key ones.

Contract

- The ability to define, articulate and present yourself as a consultant offering the knowledge and skills which are your greatest strengths and your proposed market's greatest needs.
- Enabling your targeted market, client, organisation or employer to recognise if and how their needs can be adequately, efficiently and economically met by the consultation (product) you will be providing.

- This aspect concerns the competency of agreeing a sale, a contract, or a mutual commitment to a planned course of action over a certain time, for a certain fee. This may or may not include the specification of the desired outcome for the organisation.

    Product plus **need** equals **sale**.

Connection

- Listening to your client is probably the most important competency. This includes not only what they want you to hear, but also what they do not want you to hear: issues of danger, discrimination, fear. It is vital that this competency be understood not merely as your ability to listen to the client but also the client's experience of being heard by you.
- Talking, writing, and persuasion. Whether the ethics are conscious or unconscious is not at issue here; however, the competency of articulating, explaining and persuading – what in ancient Greece was called rhetoric – *is*. This includes visual images, metaphor and presentation.
- Establishing dialogic communication. The key competency for dialogic communication between consultant and client is the ability to enter into the subjective frame of reference of the 'other' without losing the inner locus of evaluation of one's own frame of reference, one's separateness and external perspective. A steady rhythm of contact and withdrawal responsive to changing circumstances prevents confluence as well as solipsism.

    You plus **me** equals **us**.

Comprehension

- A linear, rational model of understanding organisational dynamics is useful since this is the style of thinking and learning that most people will have respect for, even though many people have experienced the failure of these models in unpredictable creative or crisis situations.
- A non-linear, intuitive model uses the knowledge, skills, attitudes and habits from areas such as art, chaos and complexity theory, quantum physics, postmodern cultural deconstruction, and so on, which are more suitable to rapidly changing circumstances and unpredictability. These models are often useful when other models have demonstrably failed.
- The consultant needs, in addition, the flexibility and range to move between these models, to judge the probable appropriateness and effectiveness for different situations.

    Left hemisphere plus **right hemisphere** equals **a whole brain**.

Conduct

- One of the most important things in consultancy is learning and pacing the *timing* of actions or interventions in terms of the natural organismic cyclic patterns. This ever-circulating pattern is variously described but usually includes punctuations around sensation, awareness, mobilisation, action, contact, climax, satisfaction and withdrawal.
- The most efficient way of implementing second-order change is to target the point in the system where the smallest effort will have the largest desirable effect, i.e. the least resistance.
- Volume control. What I mean by this is the ability to either rhythmically or appropriately adjust the force or gentleness of interventions whether these are repetitions or entirely novel.

Timing plus **spacing** equals **success**.

Caution

- The competency of refraining from action when appropriate is essential so that the consultant can create the space and opportunity for the other to take full partnership share.
- Frequent and complete periods of withdrawal by the consultant can avoid the hypnotic induction of large systems to share their assumptions, prejudices and limitations.
- Without adequate periods of rest, nourishment and replenishment from other sources, which must happen during periods of non-action in terms of the system, exhaustion with its resultant depletion of creative possibilities will ensue.

Contact plus **withdrawal** equals **health**.

Credit

- The major competency under learning how to value and assign credit lies in the capacity to use the experience to unlearn as well as learn from each consultation.
- Celebration and satisfaction are necessary for both the consultant and the system.
- When the assignment is completed, the major competency required is to let go, say farewell, and detach – sufficiently so that any new assignment is capable of being received as an entirely and unique moment.

Satisfaction plus **farewell** equals **a fresh hello**.

A checklist of competencies under each of these headings can be made to form the basis for plans for celebrating, teaching or acquiring the consultancy competencies identified in this way. The articulation of these competencies can be very useful if explored with dedication and imagination. Supported by group process work, experiential exercises based on these competencies and practice consultancy sessions with peers can anticipate problems, provide feedback and generalise this experience to ordinary work settings.

Further Reading

Adair, G. (1993). 'Scrutiny: Freud slips into the shadows', *Sunday Times*, London, 9 May.
Briggs, J. (1992). *Fractals: The Patterns of Chaos*. London: Thames and Hudson.
Briggs, J. and Peat, F. D. (1990). *Turbulent Mirror*. New York: Harper & Row.
Chambers, I. (1990). *Border Dialogues: Journeys in Postmodernity*. London: Routledge.
Clarkson, P. (1992). *Transactional Analysis Psychotherapy: An Integrated Approach*. London: Routledge.
Clarkson, P. (1994). *The Achilles Syndrome*. Cirencester: Element.
Clarkson, P. and Shaw, P. (1992). 'Human relationships at work – the place of counselling skills and consulting skills and services in organisations', *MEAD*, 23(1), 18–29
Clayton, S. (1992).'Quantum dynamics: are there metaphors for the gestalt process?', *Gestalt SouthWest News*, 29 February.
Cottone, R. R. (1988). 'Epistemological and ontological issues in counselling: Implications of social systems theory', *Counselling Psychology Quarterly*, 1(4), 357–65.
Gergen, K. (1990). 'Towards a postmodern psychology', *The Humanistic Psychologist*, 18, 23–34
Gerstein, L. H. and Shullman, S. L. (1992). Counseling psychology and the workplace: The emergence of organizational counseling psychology. In S. D. Brown and R. W. Lent (Eds.), *Handbook of Counseling Psychology*, 2nd edn, pp. 581–625. New York: John Wiley.
Gleick, J. (1989). *Chaos: Making a New Science*. London: Heinemann.
Goodman, P. S. and associates (1982). *Change in Organizations: New Perspectives on Theory, Research, and Practice*. San Francisco, CA: Jossey-Bass.
Gruber, H. (1988). 'Inching our way up Mount Olympus: The evolving systems approach to creative thinking'. In Robert J. Sternberg (Ed.), *The Nature of Creativity*. Cambridge: Cambridge University Press.
Herman, S. M. and Korenich, M. (1977). *Authentic Management: A Gestalt Orientation to Organizations and Their Development*. Reading, MA: Addison-Wesley.
Heisenberg, W. (1930). *The Physical Principles of the Quantum Theory*. New York: Dover.
Koestler, A. (1972).*The Roots of Coincidence*. London: Hutchinson.
Laing, R. D. and Esterson, A. (1972). *Leaves of Spring*. Harmondsworth, Middx: Penguin.
London, M. (1988). *Change Agents: New Roles and Innovation Strategies for Human Resource Professionals*. San Francisco, CA: Jossey-Bass.
Mandelbrot, B. B. (1974). *The Fractal Geometry of Nature*. New York: Freeman.
Morgan, G. (1986). *Images of Organization*. Beverly Hills, CA: Sage.

Moult, G. (1990). 'Under new management', *MEAD,* **21**(3), 171–82
Parsons, R. D. and Meyers, J. (1984). *Developing Consultation Skills.* San Francisco, CA: Jossey-Bass.
Peters, T. (1992). *Liberation Management: Necessary Disorganization for the Nanosecond Nineties.* London: Macmillan.
Senge, P.M. (1990). *The Fifth Discipline.* London: Century Business.
Waldrop, M. M. (1992). *Complexity: The Emerging Science at the Edge of Order and Chaos.* Harmondsworth, Middx.: Penguin.
Zohar, D. (1990). *The Quantum Self.* London: Bloomsbury.

Chapter 2
The scope of stress counselling at work

PETRŪSKA CLARKSON

The Problem

Employing organisations regularly ask questions such as:

- What is the organisation's responsibility towards its employees in cases of 'downsizing'?
- How do we know what kind of referrals to make to our in-house counselling service?
- How does our culture change programme relate to individual and corporate goals and mission statements?
- How do we begin to think about the interaction of individual and organisational stresses, distresses and potentials?
- What kind of work do you do?

The title of this chaper is just one choice of many to suit a particular moment – it could as easily have been 'The scope of psychological services in an organisation'.

Almost all such questions seem to come from a sincere but often unclear attempt to order this confusing intersecting arena of organisational and individual life. The same discussions over old ground taking up time, effort and intelligence could better be used in actually grappling with new problems and getting on with the assignment. The diagram shown in Fig. 2.1 was born in this way from repeatedly encountering the need to have a simple pictorial shape within which discussions about realistic and achievable contracts, appropriate boundaries and legitimate causes for concern could take place. It is particularly useful to prevent false expectations and to increase the chances of a clear and achievable contract.

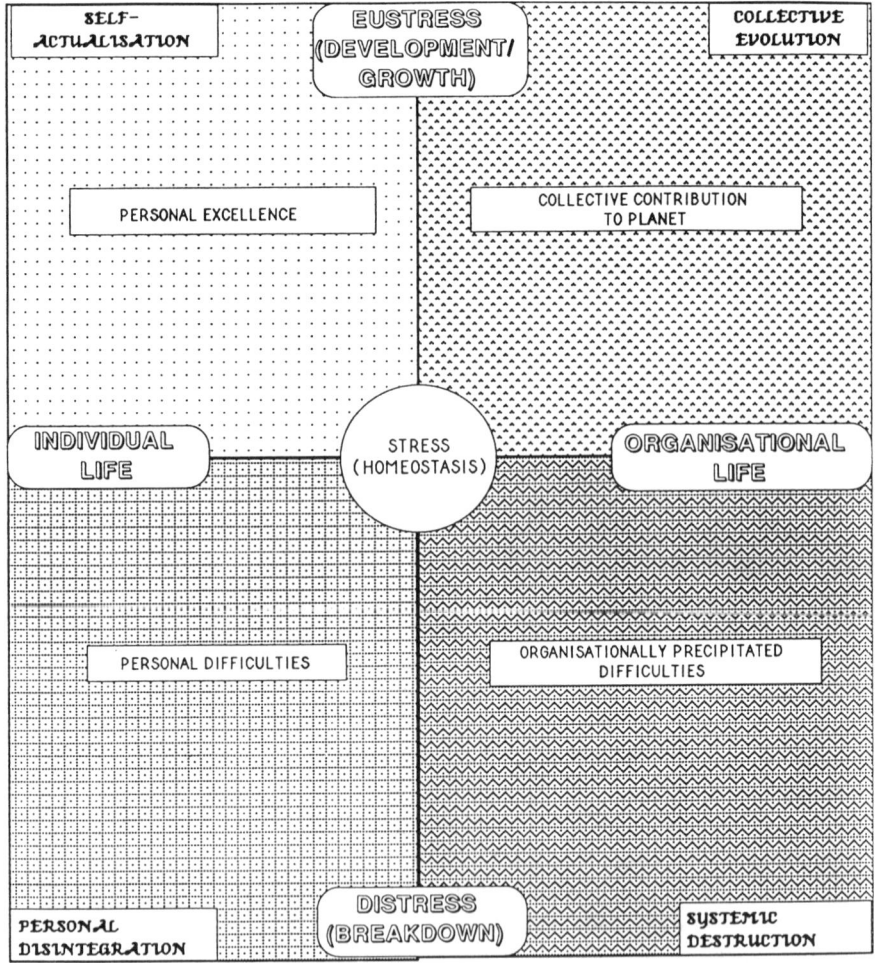

Figure 2.1

Introduction

Counselling in organisations is a rapidly growing field which is complex and challenging. According to Tittmarr, several 'U.K. Employee Counselling Programs have, as their common core philosophy, a stress-management approach' (1988, p. 223). This chapter attempts to provide a preliminary map to facilitate conceptual understanding, pragmatic decision-making and perhaps even vision in these terms. The grid shown in Fig. 2.1 provides a visual aid to this effect.

The image of going to a psychotherapist or counsellor still carries with it remnant associations of madness, sickness or weakness. In a sense this may actually be a good thing, since someone's reluctance to take on 'patient' labels often shows a commitment to solving problems and a willingness to take responsibility and action for the difficulties one is experiencing. Life offers all of us inevitable and infinitely varied challenges ranging from sudden illness to growing disillusionment with a life's vocation.

The notion of 'stress' has great popular appeal since most 'important people' suffer from stress. Some employees report that not to suffer from 'stress' would almost be embarrassing, in the same way as it might at one time have been shameful for a manager to admit to 'not being busy'. People understand that they are not necessarily weak, mad or sick when they experience psychological or emotional difficulties: they may be suffering from stress. Popular opinion is forming that almost everyone has emotional or physical responses to dealing with their everyday or unusual stresses, whether these are created in their personal lives through marital fights or in their organisational lives through the appointment of a disliked supervisor.

This growing understanding makes it acceptable for many ordinary individuals to ask for counselling or psychological information to deal with emotional, physical, interpersonal, life and work problems. In a complementary way, organisations have realised that the provision of such services to their employees is cost-effective as well as humane. Intelligent strategies to retain and improve good staff include providing resources for them, in total confidentiality, to cope with or recover from the stresses and strains of personal and organisational life in the 1990s. Counselling in organisations goes some of the way toward achieving such goals and, if stress is a useful concept toward such aims, it deserves our attention.

In the grid shown in Fig. 2.1 stress is represented as the central locus or neutral gear. (This grid is intended to be a tool and it is not intended that any of the identified divisions have absolute dividing lines or can be completely separated from each other. They naturally overlap and interlink in the way that all living systems do and it is up to the individual interpreters of the map to use it conscientiously, ethically and imaginatively.)

The abounding popular definitions of stress usually associate the notion with negative feelings and negative reactions, as if it is something to be guarded against, avoided or at most, 'managed' in a healthy way. This shows a drift from the original conceptualisations of stress, which I believe are more fruitful. Hans Selye, one of the original researchers on this venerable topic, saw it very differently. He defined it as 'the nonspecific response of the body to any demand made upon it. . . .it is immaterial whether the agent or situation we face is pleasant or unpleasant' (1975, pp. 14–15). He considered that stress is necessary for life and that the only 'unstressed' organism is a dead organism. So, *essentially stress is a value-free concept which describes the condition of a healthy, living, growing organism in interaction with its environment.*

He defined a system's homeostasis as its 'tendency to maintain a steady state despite external changes' (Selye, 1975, p. 148). 'Homeostasis' means that the body tends to maintain the same temperature, within certain limits (in a similar way to a room with a thermostat). When the body gets too hot, a negative feedback causes sweating and other physiological mechanisms to cool it down. When it gets too cold, shivering may occur; this appears to be a physiological response which tends to warm the body. In a similar way it used to be believed that people only wished to maintain the status quo or a 'steady state'. So, stress can be seen as the individual's or organism's attempts to maintain a certain homeostasis based on negative feedback.

Whether or not this stress is transformed into pleasure or pain is dependent on a great variety of factors. Psychologically, socially and physiologically it used to be believed that organisms are driven to keep restoring their equilibrium by reducing stress. Modern thinking has considerably modified this position to the idea of a *dynamic* homeostasis (Wilden, 1980) which contains the seeds of an evolutionary drive for growth and development, rather than a perennial return to baseline (Clarkson, 1991).

Selye also separated out the concept of *eustress* (based on the Greek *eu*, meaning well), which is pleasant or beneficial stress, from *distress*, which is subjectively experienced as unpleasant or even harmful. In Fig. 2.1 stress is conceptualised on the vertical axis as ranging from eustress (development) at the top end to distress (breakdown) at the lower end with the homeostatic notion of stress in the centre.

People vary in what they subjectively experience as positive or negative stress. Eustress is the pleasant, exciting experience of organismic stressors. Of course, what is one person's meat may be another person's poison. Some people thrive on tight deadlines, an excited atmosphere, even a certain level of nervous tension, whereas others would find this intolerably distressing. Alternatively, routine, predictability and security, which may be pleasantly stressing for some individuals, can be experienced by others as extremely and stressfully harmful to their long-term well-being. In my experience as consultant, the kinds of decision-making which middle managers find stressful in a negative way are experienced by autonomous senior executives, who have more control over the effects of their decisions, as pleasantly stimulating and a source of genuine satisfaction. So, the same kinds of decisions may be pleasant for some managers and distressing to others.

The horizontal axis in the illustration represents the continuum from the *individual* to the *organisation*. In this case it represents the individual at the left end and the organisation at the right. The relationship between the individual and the collective is surely one of the most vitally forming and potentially transforming vectors of human life. It is along this continuum that most individuals seek their job satisfaction, their sense of valued competency and recognition for their contribution to society whether that be running a public company or a home. From the Hawthorne studies of the 1930s (Roethlisberger and Dickson, 1939) to the child development theories of today (Stern, 1985), the human need for mastery, accomplishment and purposeful work (which is also valued by others) continues to prove central to human life. In the organisations of the next century it is likely to prove even more crucial as people seek meaning and purpose outside of themselves.

The *left half* of Fig. 2.1 delineates the area which focuses on the individual, from the pathological end of personal disintegration to the ideal end of self-actualisation. The *right half* delineates the area which focuses on the organisation, from its destruction on the pathological end to its vitally transforming role in the collective evolution of our time on the ideal end. The *bottom half* of the diagram represents areas of difficulty and potential danger for the individual and the organisation and the *upper half* areas for growth, development and evolution. Unfortunately, many organisations only concentrate on the lower part of the spectrum and appear to believe that the upper part will look after itself.

The next level of analysis involves looking at each of the quadrants. The quadrant between the individual and distress is characterised by *personal difficulties* which the individual would probably have had whether or not they worked for the particular organisation. These include vulnerability to alcohol dependence, bereavement, family tensions, an unhealthy lifestyle, for example. Where personal difficulties of an individual's life threaten or result in distress (breakdown), personal disintegration can be the outcome. In such a case, without the intervention of counselling or psychotherapeutic help, a person may end up in jail, hospital, a mental asylum or the morgue. In any event, in the short term, the employer stands to lose productivity and in the long term an employee who could have been salvaged. An employee counselling programme could have prevented such debilitating distress or aided in the recovery of the individual. Appropriate counselling strategies include individual counselling or employee assistance, as well as mental health or affective education, such as stress management, effective communication and lifestyle management programmes. For example, setting up an in-house counselling service which is confidential to the consumers of the service, on a separate site and completely independent of the usual managerial structure, to deal with increasing alcoholism and absenteeism due to marital problems of staff possibly exacerbated by relocations.

The quadrant between the organisation and distress is characterised by various degrees of *organisationally precipitated difficulties*. These involve personal stresses caused or precipitated by organisational changes or stresses. These typically may stem from threatened redundancies, re-organisations, take-overs, changes in policy or management, relocations, changes in the market position of the company, or the introduction of new technology. The stresses experienced by individual employees may or may not have been part of their individual sensitivities, but specific and identifiable factors in the organisational life are contributing to or precipitating the distressing experiences and harmful outcomes for the individuals employed by the organisation. This of course may result in burn-out (see Chapter 13).

When this is multiplied and too many employees become distressed as a result of organisational dysfunction or institutional problems, the organisation itself, along with its employees, suffers the effects and *systemic destruction* may be the outcome. Counselling, but particularly organisational consultancy of a problem-solving kind, can be of great benefit in such cases. For example, engaging in shadow consultancy to the staff members (Human Resources and Internal Consultant) in reviewing and reworking company responsibility and culture in an old family business which was still very successful, but could see that if changes were not made immediately, the future might not be so rosy at all. Few people could see why the restructuring was necessary. Fewer still were willing to lose a substantial proportion of the dollars in their pockets which would have to happen before the company profits worldwide could have re-organised at a higher level, and more fit for the future. On a planetary level, systemic breakdown is what happens when organisations destroy the resources from which they feed. Both the individuals and the collective suffer the destructive effects of such short-sighted policies and the system itself breaks down in the end. Such is still a possible outcome of the way organisations, particularly industries and deforestation drives, have harmed the planet and exploited people for gains, which in the end may prove more expensive than any of us can afford. This is different from the necessary deconstruction of transitions.

The quadrant between the individual and eustress (or growth and developmental stressors) is characterised by *individual excellence*. The individual here is characterised by a drive for mastery, competency and excellence which is probably independent of the company for which he or she works. She or he would carry their talent with them and enhance any situation to which they were committing their talents, whether these be playing cricket on the village green or developing marketing strategies for a Europe without frontiers. Such highly motivated, self-driving individuals can however, because of their very individuality and self-sufficiency, actualise themselves at the expense of their organisations. At its worst this was exemplified by the ethos of 'me first' and 'loadsamoney' where the individual reigns at the expense of the collective and the selfish altruism which Selye and myself believe to be characteristic of healthy individuals becomes perverted or distorted. An example of this was where career consultancy was offered to one exceptional individual whose personal gifts and genius were more of a problem to his employer than a benefit. In the early formation of the company, this person had been the chief mover and shaker, designing all the successful prototypes pretty much on his own and bringing many dare-devil risks off with aplomb.

In the metaphor of the author writing about organisational developmental phases who wrote *From Barbarians to Bureaucrats* (source unknown), he was one of the original barbarians, and the time for bureaucrats had arrived in his organisation. Creativity now seemed to be valued less than the ability to sit through dozens of meetings getting 34 other people to agree that it was worth spending a few dollars on a project he intuited would work – but could not prove to the accountants. He was better off out.

The quadrant between eustress and organisational life is characterised by *synergetic excellence* involving the collective (even the planet) in a way which validates both the individual and his or her organisational context. An individual is inextricably a contributing part of the whole and caring for the wider context, whether that be the company benevolent fund, social programme or ecological strategy. It is a growing conviction among individuals, organisational theorists and forecasters of megatrends that such endeavours inexorably rebound positively on the eustress quotient and the quality of life of the individuals who make the contribution. An example I have is when working as an internal consultant to a social services department and being given the assignment of developing groupwork in the area. Within a year some 54 groups were set up and running for shorter or longer periods in a great variety of settings – reminiscences groups in old people's homes, activity groups for children at risk, psychotherapy and family therapy groups, management consultancy and process groups for the top management layers.

Individuals participating in the training, the supervision and consultancy as well as the running of the groups reported enormously enhanced job satisfaction, greater benefit to clients in terms of resourcefulness and skill. Many participants also reported greater personal satisfaction in terms of their relationships with colleagues, their family members, their self-awareness and communication patterns – and their self-worth, stress resistance and, yes, even happiness.

Increasingly this appreciation is articulated in terms of companies' mission statements. These mission statements need, however, to become blood and marrow of the organisational culture and the individual's values in a coherent gestalt (Clarkson, 1989). It is unlikely that a sense of buoyant resilience under the gross and sometimes appalling stressors of our collective and international situations can be developed and maintained without the facilitation of counsellors and organisational consultants for whom these are important values and who have developed the relevant skills and vision for the task. As we move towards the twenty-first century with all its attendant confusion, anguish and complexity, we can be encouraged by the mysterious ordering principles which appear after we have exceeded our boundaries in the convoluted beauties of fractal phenomena (Gleick, 1988).

This wide perspective on the scope of counselling in organisations implies that counselling services need to embrace affective education or emotional literacy for healthy physical and emotional living as well as counselling in response to personal difficulties and organisationally induced upheaval or distressing disruption. Neither should the task end there, with short-sighted interventions or knee-jerk damage limitation. Effective companies in tune with the best current developments and on target for creative responses to the challenges of the future are also looking to widen the meaning of stress. They recruit and encourage individuals who have learnt to live their lives in the ways of 'ordinary champions'. They create organisational cultures where individuals can be enabled to find ways and means of living not only against distress, but effectively and joyfully striving for increased eustress, individually as well as collectively. Employee counselling should not be tackled on a piecemeal basis, but should be coherently and effectively integrated with assessment, training and consultancy endeavours to form part of a coherent overall strategy for the whole organisation.

References

Clarkson, P. (1989). *Gestalt Counselling in Action*. London: Sage.

Clarkson, P. (1991). 'Individuality and commonality in gestalt', *On Psychotherapy*, 1(1), 28–37.

Gleick, J. (1988). *Chaos: Making a New Science*. London: Heinemann.

Roethlisberger, F.J. and Dickson, W.J. (1939). *Management and the Worker*. Cambridge, MA: Harvard University Press.

Selye, H. (1975). *Stress Without Distress*. New York: Signet.

Stern, D. (1985). *The Interpersonal World of the Infant*. New York: Basic Books.

Tittmarr, H. G . (1988). 'Counselling for problem drinking: employee assistance programs versus employee counselling programs (a commentary)', *Counselling Psychology Quarterly*, 1 (2 &3), 221–8.

Wilden, A. (1980). *System and Structure* (2nd edn). London: Tavistock.

Chapter 3
Redundancy counselling

PETRŪSKA CLARKSON

The Problem

I was requested to do a three-day training for outplacement counsellors of a large multinational consultancy company. This outplacement service would be exclusively staffed by personnel from the parent company who had all individually been made redundant from their previous jobs, but were offered the opportunity of becoming redundancy counsellors instead. I was given three days to do the training of these people. I objected on ethical grounds. Being made redundant was experienced by people as a shock, a kind of bereavement, certainly a lack of meaning. I did not believe that three days could equip ex-accountants with the basics of the skills necessary to assist others in dealing with this process, much less themselves. Someone else might try, I would not.

The contract was renegotiated to 21 days to include theory, skills training, personal awareness work and supervision of cases. The cultural emphasis was on selling, selling, selling. Time spent learning about the job was considered a waste – it was more important to be out there and do business. The training was done with fine people of an extremely wide spectrum of interest and ability. The fact that some individuals felt superior to others was based on familiarity with the Egan material on client-centred counselling, so it seemed essential to find a model which all could experience as fresh, each one bringing their own previous experiences to it. The training was conducted in a constant atmosphere of stress, worry and important managerial meetings with the next corporate layer up.

The Cycle of Human Experience

In this work of training people in counselling skills to help individuals deal with being made redundant, the idea of a cycle of human experience has been found useful. This helps trainees understand the different phases and reactions of individuals to major life events, such as redundancy, and also to locate a set of counselling skills at different points on the cycle.

As human beings, we are all constantly involved in making sense of our experience of the world. Poets, mystics and philosophers have characterised experience as having a fundamentally cyclical quality.

> We shall not cease from exploration
> And the end of all our exploring
> Will be to arrive where we started
> And know the place for the first time
>
> (T.S. Eliot, *The Four Quartets*)

The same insights are often expressed in folk wisdom, such as 'What goes around comes around', and *'Plus ça change, plus c'est la même chose'*. This cyclical quality can be seen at all levels of reality – cellular, individual, group, organisational, societal, planetary, cosmological, etc.

Psychologists and biologists are looking at the basic life processes they study as having the shape of a cycle or a wave. We breathe in and out and in again. We eat and drink and eliminate, and then eat and drink again. We become sexually aroused, engage in lovemaking, come to a climax and then start getting interested in something else, like sleeping. However, in time, we'll probably start feeling like making love again. We start a project, take it through to completion and usually then start something else. It has been well documented that economic conditions have a way of coming round again. Productive managerial groups can be observed having natural work cycles, of generating the data they need, making sense of this, acting, following through their actions to a satisfying conclusion, and then moving on to the next task.

This also appears to be true of fashion – one year platform shoes are in, then they disappear from favour and then they emerge again. Civilisations rise and fall and sometimes rise again, even if in a slightly altered form. As long as we live, this cycle continues.

The purpose of learning about natural cycles is to provide people with an organismic or natural inner map to guide them, or remind them, of the natural healthy rhythms of life and healthy living things, and to alert them to when things are likely to go wrong. It may also help in identifying where and when things are going wrong, and what and how to prevent problems or to remedy them in good time.

Learning about and using the cycle as a template for human learning or change processes has been found particularly useful for people in the helping professions, to guide them through the labyrinth of the counselling process. It should never be used in a rigid, unimaginative, impersonal way, but only in the way it makes sense and meaning for the individual. Theories are meant to serve us, and not the other way around. However, it is important to realise that the cycle itself is not a theory in the usual sense of the word. It is more basic than theory. It is a shape created by nature. It is a biological sequence which does not need to be proved, because each one of us experiences the true reality of it every time we enjoy a satisfactory meal or complete a journey or reach a target.

Health and Disease in Natural and Human Cycles

Nature follows cyclical or wavelike processes, not linear ones. Spring follows winter which follows autumn, which follows summer, and so on. The spontaneous uninterrupted flow from one part of the cycle to another is a characteristic of all healthy systems, whether the systems are ecosystems, families, individual human beings, or animals.

Of course it does not always happen this way. Sometimes there is an interruption in the cycle and the natural process of movement becomes disturbed. This could be temporary, acute, where the system maybe faces a major crisis, or chronically long-term, resulting in stagnation and, ultimately, death.

In human beings, blocks to this natural cyclical process often result in disease. This can be expressed on a physical level. For example, there may be only intake and no output, as in when the kidneys fail to eliminate. Or there is only output, and no input into a system, as with individuals in the caring professions who 'burn out', and workers who keep working without ever taking breaks or taking holidays, who may find themselves exhausted and unable to continue functioning.

Phases of the Cycle

Although the cycle is a continuous process, it is helpful to distinguish different phases, as a way of understanding what is particularly important at each phase. By dividing the cycle into phases, this does not mean of course that they are always distinct and separate. It is not possible to draw rigid dividing lines where one stops and another starts; they flow into one another.

To discuss the stages separately helps us understand the different emphases over time, not to suggest, for example, that at 2.15 p.m. one period ends and another begins. This is the same as in group dynamics. We know that groups go through the phases of forming, storming, norming, performing and mourning, for example. This is the general shape of group development. Most people who have studied or participated consciously in groups have observed and experienced this shifting of focus over time. Yet it would be really hard to say at this particular moment the group started storming and stopped forming. Yet, of course, sometimes it can be very clear, as for example we sometimes know when winter has ended and spring begun.

The phases are:
- *Sensation* – a physiological response either to a need arising from within, e.g. a pang, or a cold shiver; or due to impact from the environment, e.g. the feel of different textures, a change in the economic climate.
- *Awareness* – the meaning and significance that we attach to the sensations, e.g. realising that our pangs are of hunger, not of jealousy, and that our shiver is due to fear, that the name of the game is downsizing.
- *Preparation* – preparing to act on the basis of the thoughts and feelings generated by our awareness. It is similar to mobilisation, getting our energies ready to act, all geared up to move into action.
- *Action* – the actual execution of the act, the implementation of the culture change programme, the appointment of a new board, the making of the telephone call.
- *Completion* (contact) – refers to the moment(s) of climax, of completion, of bringing the action to a satisfactory conclusion, when the organism and environment connect.
- *Satisfaction* – has to do with the subjective feelings of satisfaction, looking back on the task accomplished with pleasure, enjoyment in retrospect, even as it begins to fade.
- *Ending* (withdrawal) – concerns finishing, saying goodbye or farewell, letting go in order to go forward, leaving one task behind in order to begin to create the space for the next one to emerge.

The time period of the cycle can vary; it may take us minutes, as in making a cup of tea, to realise we are thirsty, knowing that exactly what we want is a cup of tea rather than a gin and tonic, and making and enjoying the tea – or it may take us a lifetime, as we move through the phases of birth, childhood, youth, adulthood, old age and death.

The Therapeutic Process of Counselling

Whatever people bring to counselling, there is always task as well as process – or a *what?* as well as a *how?* So, whether people come to counselling as a result of being made redundant in the organisation, or for whatever other reason, the content may be different but the basis pattern of the counselling process will be the same.

Using the natural cycle capitalises on people's natural need for recovery from physical or psychological injury and their need for growth and self-actualisation. The cycle is the basic shape of human experience and as such it underlies most effective counselling as well. It may describe the shape of a single satisfactory session or a successfully completed series of sessions. For example, from the initial consultation sessions with a person who has been made redundant through to where they have been successfully and satisfactorily found another, perhaps better job, more

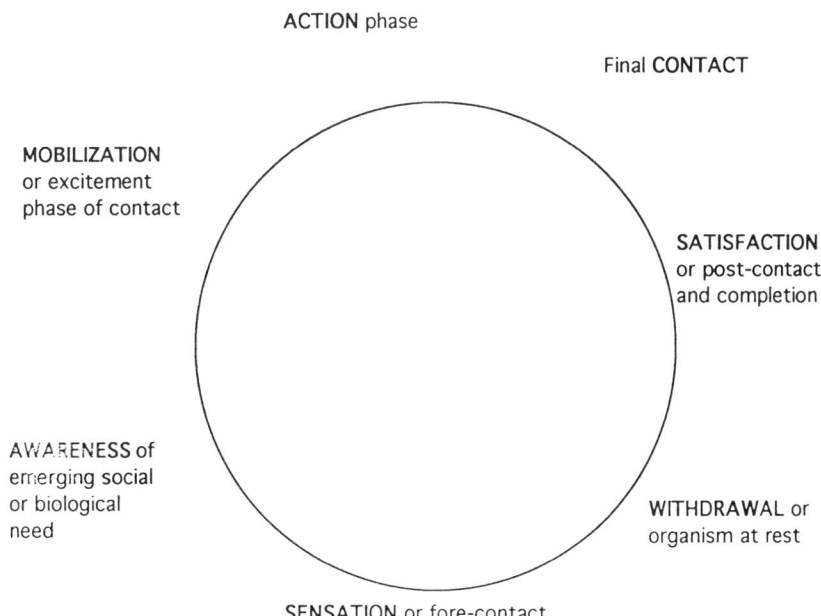

Figure 3.1 Cycle of gestalt formation and destruction

suited to their personality and likes and dislikes. It is in the nature of healthy organisms to have needs and to seek to take these to fulfilment and satisfaction before repeating the cycle again, perhaps in another form, with a different desire. It is not unusual that someone may reach the summit in one ambition or profession and then seek to develop themselves or their skills afresh in something entirely different. In one case, a man was made redundant without major financial penalty and he found that what he really wanted to do was to become a gardener: his life's satisfactions were vastly improved once he was released from the daily nine-to-five office grind. Figure 3.1 shows the cycle of Gestalt formation and destruction, and Figure 3.2 gives some indication of permissions, encouragements or signposts which individuals or counsellors can use to facilitate the smooth and satisfactory completion of people's natural cycles.

The Concept of Unfinished Business

In the previous section I dealt with the healthy way in which human beings' complete cycles, whether they be the rhythm of waking and sleeping, playing and working, creation or separation. Unfortunately, life is not always so satisfactory.

It has been proved that people not only have biological needs to complete the cycle of experience, but also psychological and even

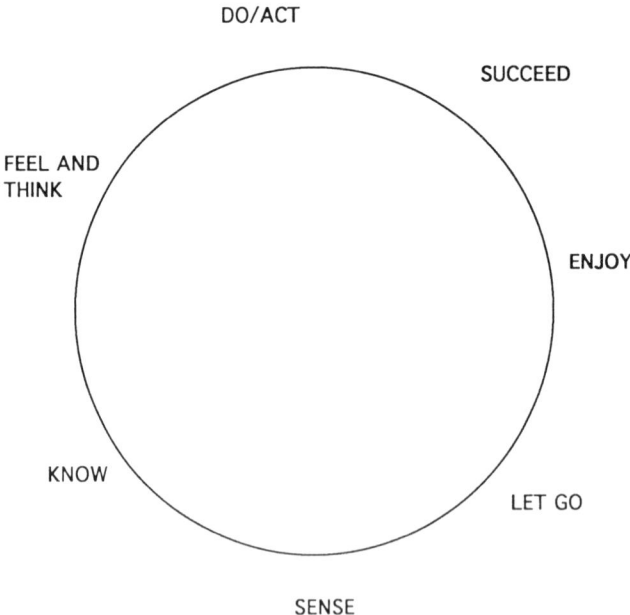

Figure 3.2 Cycle of gestalt formation and destruction with permissions (Tudor, 1991)

perceptual needs. When there is something we wanted to say in retort to a put-down remark, but we didn't, it often keeps coming back. Sometimes you go over and over what you would have wanted to say. The French have a phrase for it – *l'esprit d'escalier* – the wisdom of the staircase. There is an apocryphal story of either Mozart or Beethoven who was sleeping in a house where upstairs someone played most of a concerto, but not the final chords. The composer could not sleep and remained frustrated until he had gone upstairs and played the final chords, thus finishing the gestalt of the concerto. Only then could he relax.

This sense of incompleteness, whether emotional or psychological, is what is referred to as 'unfinished business'. One of the biggest problems in redundancy counselling is all the unfinished business people have had to leave behind – the unsaid anger, the unheard distress, the embarrassed goodbyes instead of the flowing of vintage friendships and so on. The natural cycle of their expectations that their employment and career needs would be met has been interrupted, sometimes with the shocking impact of news of a bereavement. Of course for many people it is a very serious loss. Work, or a feeling that you are making a meaningful contribution to the world, is one of the three major factors in human health and happiness. (How one feels about oneself and one's relationships being the other two.)

Interruptions to the Cycle: Their Usefulness as Coping Mechanisms

Of course we cannot always complete our natural cycles. Sometimes it is better to bite back an angry retort, to hit a cushion instead of a person, to override a temporary feeling of drowsiness or fatigue in order to get a job done rather than just giving in to the natural impulse. In such cases human beings have ways of interrupting or blocking the cycle. These blocks can appear at any stage and they are all useful under certain circumstances if they are consciously chosen, adapted to the current situation and in accord with the person's long-term needs and aspirations (see Figure 3.3).

The blocks are:

- *Numbness* (more technically called desensitisation). It is perfectly healthy, and sometimes essential, for people to be numb in certain situations. An athlete wanting to win a race may need to override the pain from a blistered foot. It is a natural response for people to go numb in some way (or avoid feeling) when they are in shock, whether that shock is psychological, such as suddenly being fired, or physical, such as losing a limb in a bomb attack.
- *Avoidance* (more technically called deflection). It is important to be able to avoid toxic stimuli from our environment such as destructive criticism, scapegoating, or the sound of jackhammers impinging on a meeting when there are important decisions to be made. Sometimes it is better to ignore a hurtful or disparaging remark or to reject a false accusation than to deal with it directly.
- *Absorption* or swallowing whole (more technically called introjection). When we begin to learn anything there is often a period where it is necessary and healthy to simply believe what the instructor has to tell you and to follow their directions, for example about something like parachute jumping. This applies to a job or situation of any complexity. Once one has learnt the art, it is easier to disagree and find one's own way independently.
- *Anticipation* (more technically called fantasy projection). It is natural and essential that people use learning from their past experiences in order to anticipate similar situations in future. In applying to join a new management team, it is very useful to rememember what it was like joining other teams before and to anticipate certain feelings, group patterns and individual behaviours. It is a normal part of learning. It is the dreams and fantasies of the future which become the blueprints of successful plans.
- *Self-criticism* or self-nurture (more technically called retroflection). Sometimes the natural learning cycle needs to be interrupted to get feedback or support. When others, for example the manager or the group, will not accept it, it may be better to 'bite back' the angry

outburst and think about how one could have avoided getting into the difficult situation in the first place.
- *Self-consciousness* (more technically called egotism). Although self-conciousness can be excessive, a certain amount of self-awareness is essential for a healthy person to grow and to learn and to thrive. It is in a way 'by watching oneself doing something' that one can learn and improve any skill, from filling in forms to developing pan-European marketing strategies.
- *Merging* (more technically called confluence). Sometimes it is healthy and important to suspend one's own desires, wants and ideas and, so to speak, blend with others for a while to achieve a common goal or share a common feeling. A feeling of 'team spirit' or mutual support for a child in difficulty between two divorced parents – when it is temporary and not destructive to any of the parties involved – does not have to mean a loss of indentity or individuality. It is often people who are willing to merge with others for a brief while, who can have empathy for others and help or lead them most effectively.

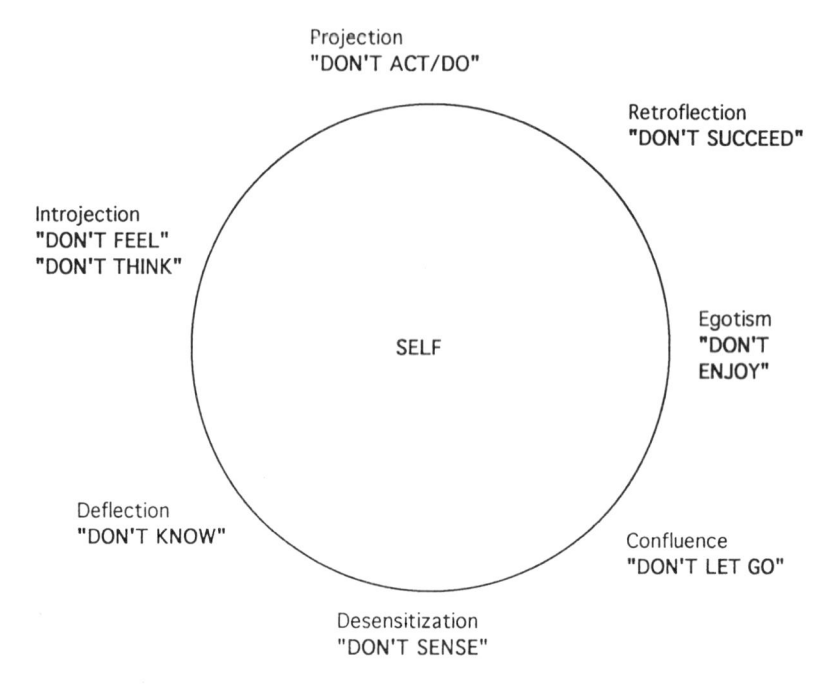

Figure 3.3 Cycle of gestalt formation and destruction with diagrammatic examples of boundary disturbances at each phase (Tudor, 1991)

When Healthy Interruptions Become Dysfunctional Blocks

Indeed, looking at human problems and counselling, a healthy natural cycle which can become blocked or interrupted can be a more humane and empowering way of working than looking for psychiatrically sounding diagnoses, for example. Counselling is them perceived as the enabling of another person to get back in touch with their own self-healing growth-seeking drive.

So, temporary numbness, avoidance, absorption (or swallowing whole), anticipation (future fantasy), self-criticism/self-nurture, self-consciousness or merging may all be relevant, appropriate and functional responses to the threat or the fact of being made redundant. They can serve a temporary self-protective function as they do in natural disasters, war or other extreme human conditions such as childhood can be.

But, all these blocks or interrruptions to the natural cycle discussed above can become dysfunctional and pathological disturbances

- when they are inappropriately used
- when they become chronically painful patterns of response
- when they are habitually used without awareness or consciousness.

So, people can continue use any of these self-protective devices after the danger has passed or without choice as a characteristic way of being in the world. They may end up cripped in emotional or physical ways and unable to respond creatively and effectively to changing conditions. If all the energy of the system is tied up in defending against feeling a past injury, there can be no recovery and no intelligent stress-free response to new challenging situations. A new job, a new lifestyle, a new location, a new set of friends – all these need a human being in high functioning order, ready to learn from the past, to anticipate the future indeed – but constantly willing and able to update their information and their learning in line with new data and new conditions. This is the meaning of survival of the fittest as Darwin meant it – not survival of the strongest, but survival of those most capable of adapting creatively to rapidly changing conditions. Figure 3.4 can be used as a summary of the material discussed so far. It combines the cycle of gestalt formation and destructuring with the stages of personal transition from Kubler-Ross (1969) and the negative and positive indications at each of the different stages of the cycle developed by Patricia Shaw and Paul Roberts with myself.

Unblocking Your Client

In working from this model with people coming about any kind of difficulty, it is important to help them to negotiate their natural grief recovery

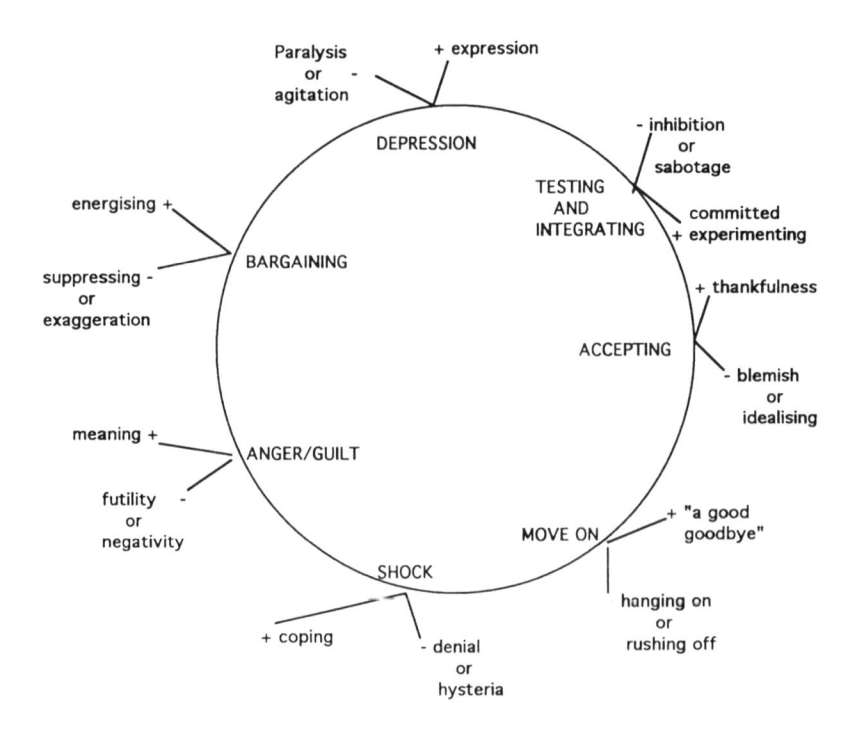

Figure 3.4 Cycle of gestalt formation and destruction with links to stages of personal transition and positive/negative manifestation.

or learning cycle – to support and facilitate their own natural drive for healing and health. In many cases all that is required is an empathetic listener who affirms and values the experience of the person who has been made redundant for example, helps them to collect and clarify their options and choices and supports them in the implementation and evaluation of these actions. The more problematical times come when the client 'gets stuck' at some point on the cycle or seem unable to move beyond it – those times when the natural drive for health is damaged or blocked.

Then it becomes of vital to identify where on the cycle they are stuck and perhaps even to use specific techniques for unblocking the energy or finishing the unfinished gestalt. Some of these techniques are more fully discussed in my book *Gestalt Counselling in Action* (Clarkson, 1989). The course material developed for this intervention exists as an unpublished manuscript and worksheets, but space limitations prevent me from exploring it further here. Training can be provided at introductory, intermediate and advanced levels with guidelines for when and under what conditions to refer to other agencies or other professionals with different or more specialised competencies. For a sample worksheet, see Table 3.1. Clearly this model has been found useful in the specialised area of outplacement counselling, but it also has a myriad other applications: for example in organisational consultancy, general counselling and psychotherapy.

Table 3.1

Theory (1)	Transition Task	Normal Healthy Response	Acute Abnormal Response (Short-term)	Chronic Abnormal Response (Long-term)	Gift/ Talent/ Qualities	Basic Interventions Essential Skills	Moderate Interventions Further Development	Highly Skilled Interventions
S	TO SENSE e.g.	Desensit-isation	Numbness Loss of focus. Loss of concentration Feeling little or nothing. Keep going for a short time as though nothing has happened. Sense of external unreality. Loss of memory.	Low grade depression and listlessness. Bored, blasé, world-weary May have pale face, be expression-less. Withdrawn Unmoved	Will not panic under stress. Creative dreamer.	Listening carefully and reflecting back what you see and hear in a clear, simple, descriptive way. Showing empathy. Unconditional acceptance. Provide sensorily rich environment -comfortable chairs -space to move colour, objects flowers, paintings -privacy and confidentiality. Be there - awake, alert, available.	Helping clients to 'ground' themselves in their senses, (dealing with shock). Encourage them to move. Contact them clearly. -use simple direct questions -focus on present and immediate situation. -use their name.	Use creative media. -drawing on large sheets -modelling with plasticene. -breathing exercises -anchoring techniques. Crisis intervention.
E	To take in the data.							
N	To notice.							
S	To register events.							
A								
T								
I								
O								
N								

References

Clarkson, P. (1989). *Gestalt Counselling in Action.* London: Sage.
Kubler-Ross, E. (1969). On Death and Dying. New York: Macmillan.
Tudor, K. (1991). 'Integrating Gestalt in children's groups', *British Gestalt Journal*, 1, 21–27.

Further Reading

Bridges, W. (1980). Transitions. Reading, MA: Addison-Wesley.
Critchley, B. and Casey, D. (1989). 'Organisations get stuck too', *Leadership and Organization Development Journal*, 10(4), 3–12.
Myers, R. A. and Cairo, P. C. (1992). 'Counseling and career adjustment', in S. D. Brown and R. W. Lent (eds) *Handbook of Counseling Psychology* (2nd edn), pp. 549–580. New York: John Wiley.

Chapter 4
The differential outcomes of organisational change

PETRŪSKA CLARKSON

The Problem

There is an awareness that the design and implementation of change interventions in an organisation can have a variety of outcomes ranging from the satisfying and effective to the disastrous. How to evaluate the inputs of organisational consultants, programmes or changes? Why do programmes *feel* good, but *do* little good in the end? How to prevent paying out vast amounts of time and money for programmes which will have little, no or devastating effect?

This chapter identifies possible outcomes of organisation consultancy interventions: *enhanced functioning, making progress, casualty, disillusionment* and *fake change*. It comes from experience, speculation and the lessons of myth and legends. It is based on the notion that organisations are individuals writ large – the same ideas applied to psychotherapy won a prize for contribution to theory in Transactional Analysis in 1988. It could have been written in any other theoretical language – first-order and second-order systems, psychoanalytic, archetypal Jungian – or in the idiosyncratic and unique words, images and language of the individuals and collective which constitute the temporary dynamic whole we call the organisation.

Introduction

One of the central assumptions of organisation development is clearly that organisations can be helped to change, through purposeful intervention, towards enhanced business performance, more effective internal functioning and greater employee satisfaction. This implies both first-order evolutionary change and second-order revolutionary change.

The parallel with change at the level of the individual system is both with counselling, through which an individual is enabled and facilitated to use existing personality resources in order to live more creatively and satisfyingly (evolutionary change), and with psychotherapy, where destructuring and reconstructing of the personality may be required, before an individual can reconnect with their natural self-actualising potential (revolutionary change).

At the level of organisational change we are looking at psychological organisation development interventions such as team building, education, communication enhancement or conflict mediation (the consultant as 'organisational counsellor') and those major initiatives which involve large-scale restructuring of a company's mission, culture and organisation (the consultant as 'organisational therapist') without which decline in a changing marketplace is inevitable.

Recognising and distinguishing genuine change as opposed to other possible outcomes of psychotherapeutic intervention which may masquerade as the real thing has intrigued and puzzled psychologists and psychotherapists for several decades. This is as pertinent a concern for organisation development practitioners from any discipline, executives and managers who are seeking to initiate or help organisational change which is genuine, stable under stress and which can provide a fertile and resilient ground for future growth.

This chapter discusses and illustrates five faces of change in organisations. Each of these faces of change will be discussed in systemic terms with their own frames of reference including organisational motivations for seeking or avoiding future changes, characteristic response patterns and differing capacities in managing stress and distress. Each is associated with an archetypal or mythological image which may aid the consultant in distinguishing, defining and recognising the five types of outcome. Archetypal legends are often useful since the image or the story can be more precise than many lengthy explanations, scientific or business administration dissertations on the topic.

The five faces of change are

- *real change* (leading to enhanced functioning)
- *no change* (or making progress)
- *impossible change* (leading to disillusionment)
- *destructive change* (leading to casualties)
- *fake change* (leading to the illusion of autonomy and growth).

Other names may be better suited, but these are the ones I used first.

Real Change

Here an entire organisational system can identify and break out of limiting ways of working, of interacting with its environment, of depriving its operations, of deploying its resources. Its culture can truly change. This kind of change means that organisations can change entirely and put a new show on the road with new characters, new roles and a new plot and payoff (Berne, 1972, p. 362).

This kind of change also has a number of phenomenological characteristics. Organisations that have made such fundamental changes of character and destiny often report an 'ad lib' quality to their lives and relationships. They no longer know what to say and their networks frequently undergo considerable oscillation, for example there are new colleagues and old friends no longer seem so close or supportive of the new way of being.

The organisation which has 'flipped in' has a frame of reference where changing is experienced a satisfying and autonomous. Not only are changes imposed by the environment or natural cycle welcomed a learning opportunities, such organisations also seek change and growth in continuing ways. They develop and nourish their own particular needs and levels for stimulation and excitement, complexity and diversity which Selye (1957) referred to as 'eustress'.

The change process itself is experienced as energising and they are proactive and creative. Such organisations act upon their world. They have overcome the subjective learned helplessness (Miller and Seligman, 1976) which reinforces the powerlessness of habit-bound organisations. Research (Kiev and Cohn, 1949) has shown that senior levels of management derive satisfaction from working under stresses which middle managers may experience as distress. It is hypothesised that this is due to the feeling that their decisions actually affect the outcomes they initiate.

Characteristically change continues to be important in such organisations, but it is essentially post-pathological; away from curing the pathology towards growth. It has to do with responding adaptively and creatively to life's stress (Holmes and Rahe, 1967) and progressing with increasing autonomy and assurance through developmental stages (Erikson, 1968; Levinson, 1978).

Real and lasting change is achieved when the organisation development intervention is stable under ordinary and extreme stress. Creativity becomes the natural response to environmental demands, instead of whining or paralysis. Some vicissitudes of life such as bereavement, loss of jobs, natural disasters, war and other unpredictable events can challenge the organisational change profoundly.

The archetypal image is Odysseus. He travelled thousands of miles to win a war, returning home via many adventures with cons, crooks and concubines, misfortune and adversity. He is reinstated on his throne in his kingdom where his wife had waited patiently and faithfully for him largely due to his resilience, imagination and resourcefulness in changing as the circumstances (of life, war and peace) changed.

No Change – Making Progress

'Making progress' is a kind of change that has incremental or pendulum characteristics. Its like 'three steps forward, two steps back', banal, 'neither here-nor-there really' or what employees in the washrooms or the pub often describe as 'going through the motions again'.

This outcome of organisation development interventions is not a true change at all, but mere fluctuation which may be mistaken for real change. This type of 'change' is a masquerade of living creatively within very narrow norms of maintaining banal organisational scripts or patterns. By moving three steps forward, two back and two steps forward, three back, an organisation can give the impression that there is movement or progress, but a hard contractual check over any length of time will prove that in fact no significant long-term stable change has indeed been accomplished. Changing requires not only the willingness to take full responsibility, but also courage.

Organisations which feel that they have accomplished change but have in fact made progress usually place great value on the maintenance of a single world view and tend to find reinforcing experiences which support the future avoidance of both positively and negatively valued stresses. Even in fantasy, changing or the stimulus to change, is perceived a negative, destabilising and therefore undesirable. Their goal is homeostasis or stability within very narrow but predictable limits. If an employee doesn't have the right attitude they're out. The right attitude means agreement with the current version of the emperor's clothes. Organisation development may end up by widening the limits somewhat, but the basic restrictions on autonomy and creativity are stretched or redefined, not changed.

However, making progress obviously has some value. Such first-order, three steps forward, two steps back incremental kind of changes have their place and are certainly better than a headlong rush into catastrophe which results in the organisation responding by disintegration or catastrophe. Organisations need to change at the pace and rhythm and depth they can manage and not according to their consultant's need for stimulation or peacefulness (excitement or an easy life).

A characteristic response to change is that this system is in a continual state of stress, holding bound and unbound energy, archaic experiences and the influence of rules, guidelines, policy documents and suchlike, while at the same time avoiding true contact with the here-and-now experience which could potentially destabilise a delicate balance. Essentially these organisations are chronically stressed, rigid in their attitudes. Employees frequently experience a chronic low level of fatigue and a minimum tolerance for deviance, uncertainty or ambiguity.

The response pattern of organisations that are making progress is recognisably *reactive* to the initiative of others, the environment or habit. These organisations are essentially passive in response to stimuli from the environment and from others and do not actualise their own pattern. They often accumulate awareness at the expense of real change. There is no pro-activity or what there is is stereotyped, predictable to the competition and lacking vitality and novelty.

The archetypal image here is that of Sisyphus – condemned forever to roll a stone uphill and just when he accomplished that, it would roll down and he would have to start all over again and again, for ever.

Impossible Change – Disillusionment

This is the outcome of organisation development interventions when the organisation ends up destroyed in a negative way. (I say this in order to make allowance for organisations which are destructured or dissolved in a healthy way. The dissolution of the Whole Earth catalogue (Phillips, 1974) is an instructive example of the latter.) Misguided Utopian hope is indeed one of the major problems to which organisational consultants and their employing organisations are particularly susceptible. Over-idealisation can lead to a concern to achieve the seeming impossible at the cost of the truly possible.

Much disappointment can be avoided by recognising and then confronting wisely and timely the realism and achievability of goals and expectations (which may be so out of awareness that they may only become known toward the end or after the culture change or business process engineering intervention). This kind of disillusionment occurs where either overtly or covertly the outcome of the interventions is confused at an unconscious level with the attainment of omnipotence, irresistibility or practical immorality. The desired change is essentially inappropriate.

Furthermore, even after the huge investment of time, thought, emotion and money, life continues to be life. A change in the international monetary system affects everyone, the price of crude oil rises, new legislation makes labour costs unsupportable.

Consultants can avoid getting involved with a fruitless quest for inappropriate change by (amongst other procedures) clarifying contracts, checking third party involvement, learning about the field. Characteristic of misdiagnosis of achieved or non-achieved organisational change is that the system is simply not designed for the function required of it and so suffers breakdown.

Organisations caught in this kind of system cannot tolerate attempting to change in an organismically impossible way, nor the stress of attempting to maintain such an impossible change. Disillusionment may then mar or ruin a possible organisational change by the vain effort of seeking to change the impossible. Flying so high that nobody can get there results in scorched wings at best, or death by drowning at worst.

The archetypal image of Icarus encapsulates the organisation's experience in this case. His father made him beautiful feathered wings with which to fly and fly he did, but his ambitions drew him too close to the burning sun. His wings melted and he died flaming in the Aegean sea.

Destructive Change

This outcome of organisation development intervention occurs in a system when a change to the organisation is not just destabilising but also disintegrating. Unlike Icarus' change, the desired change is possible but it is under the influence of Mortido (Federn, 1977), the death instinct. The system can neither tolerate it nor creatively respond to it. It results most frequently from mistimed interventions, inadequate anticipation or dysfunctional planning.

The motivating frame of reference is that the world does not correspond to the ideal or desired view of it. The stimulus to change is imagined as noxious and the organisation may insist that unless homeostasis is maintained on its own terms, destruction will result. The response pattern is sabotage or flight. It could be referred to as a casualty. I think in order to minimise this likelihood many organisations employ a number of different inputs, trainers, consultants and so on without much communication or coordination. In this way the risk of disintegration is minimised, but so too is the possibility of second-order change which faces the risks and takes them well.

Change that strips away defences without the simultaneous provision of protection, skills, knowledge and resources can result in such disintegration. It is important to attend to the impact of the change on the organisation's psycho-sociological networks, the relearning or acquiring of developmentally impaired skills, maintenance procedures, and re-inforcement practice for stability under stress. An inordinate fear of chaos, turbulence or the upheaval and unpredictability which accompanies creativity can precipitate and worsen panic reactions to what may be just a temporary phase as an organisation re-adjusts to a second-order or profound systemic change.

On the other hand, no matter how conscientiously a consultant honours an organisation's contract, there is always still the possibility that the organisation may be more heavily invested in forwarding the destructive script than in creative change. As is well known, the consultant gets blamed easily and quickly for organisational failure, which is the very condition that made the work impossible.

The archetypal image is that of Medea – the vengeful Greek queen who killed her children and fed them to her husband in rage, destroying all about her without mercy.

Fake Change – The Illusion of Autonomy

This type of outcome is a kind of pseudo-conversion – the belief that the change is fundamental when it is actually cosmetic. Changes, particularly culture changes in these cases have an introjected quality – as if they have been swallowed whole and then regurgitated, not digested. It concerns the superficial adoption of new behaviour and belief systems, even a new language, in the service of maintaining the old disempowered system and preventing any genuine disturbing change.

The fantasy is that autonomy has been achieved. There is redecision without a fundamental transformation or a reorganisation at a deep structural level has occurred. But it hasn't. Employees have keyrings and desk calendars which have slogans on such as 'Put customers first', but it does not really mean anything to them. They have overadapted because that may be the way to keep the job, not because of any thorough personal conviction. As the saying goes: 'A man convinced against his will, is of the same opinion still'. The test lies in how the organisation responds to or initiates the next set of learnings or change. A reversion to old patterns often indicates that the previous change had been false, superficial or cosmetic, not an integrated experience in developing changing skills or learning attitudes.

The archetypal image is that of Oedipus. He thought he had it all sussed out, but every time he tried to escape his destiny, destiny caught up with him. As soon as you think you know what's going on and that you're in control – you're probably not. An organisation that is too sure of itself, can be sure only that life will bring a sudden different lesson sooner or later.

When discussing potential assignments with clients, and evaluating previous organisational interventions of other or the same consultants, this framework gives us a common language, images and options. It can prevent unrealistic expectations. It seems most useful in reflecting on past experiences as one prepares for the new.

For the consultant, the prayer of St Francis of Assisi can be a guiding motto in sorting out different kinds of intervention, realistic expectations, possible outcomes and the skilfulness, flexibility and resourcefulness of Odysseus:

> Lord, Give me the courage to change to change the things I can;
> The serenity to accept the things I cannot change;
> And the wisdom to know the difference.

References

Berne, E. (1972). *What Do You Say After You Say Hello?* New York: Grove Press.
Erikson, E.H. (1968). *Heredity, Youth and Crisis.* New York: Norton.
Federn, P. (1977). *Ego Psychology and the Psychoses.* London: Maresfield Reprints

(first published 1928).
Holmes, T.H. and Rahe, R.H. (1967). 'The social readjustment rating scale', *Journal of Psychosomatic Research*, **11**, 213-18.
Kiev, A. and Cohen, V. (1949). *Executive Stress: An AMA Survey Report*. New York: Amacom.
Levinson, D.J. (1978). *The Seasons of a Man's Life*. New York: Ballantine.
Miller, W.C. and Seligman, M.E.P. (1976). 'Depression and learned helplessness in Man', *Journal of Abnormal Psychology*, **84**, 228-38.
Phillips M. (1974). The Seven Laws of Money. Menlo Park, CA: World Wheel and Random House.
Selye, H. (1957). *The Stress of Life*. London: Low and Brydone.

Futher Reading

Bandler, R. and Grinder, J. (1982). *Reframing: Neuro-Linguistic Programming and the Transformation of Meaning*. Moab, UT: Real People Press.
Watzlawick, P., Weakland, J. H. and Fisch, R. (1974). *Change: Principles of Problem Formation and Problem Resolution*. New York: Norton.

Chapter 5
Prioritising organisational interventions –
a diagnostic framework

What goes wrong in management consultancy, and some pointers to how to minimise it

PETRŪSKA CLARKSON and KAMIL KELLNER

The Problem

Trainers are often asked to train, consultants to consult, counselling psychologists to counsel in situations which are less than ideal if not bluntly impossible. By identifying different layers of difficulty and responding appropriately to each, as well as clarifying in advance when an effort is likely to prove worthless, consultants and organisations, participants and trainers have a better chance of getting needs met for the individuals and the corporations involved. Trainers who try and train managers who are pre-occupied with being 'downsized' before the end of the financial year need to review and rearrange or reframe training priorities. Often when the consultant cannot figure out why everything seems to be going wrong, it is because it is. This framework helps practically in many situations, including emergencies. Furthermore, it is simple and understandable and a good basis for deciding respective responsibilities and priorities for action.

Introduction

In this article we discuss a framework which many management consultants, managers and organisational developers have found useful. Clarkson first developed it in the 1980s. Here we specifically describe it as a simple diagnostic tool to help both experienced and novice consultants working in organisations. It is of particular value in finding out quickly what is (or went) wrong and how to avoid similar problem(s) in future.

Organisational behaviour and management consultancy are such complex fields that the more you learn, the more options for action open up. Taking the next decision can get increasingly difficult. Of all the many choices facing management consultants, the most strategically important is probably how to prioritise – what is most important in a specific situation, how to select what to do next, to which factors to give most urgent attention.

Consultancy literature offers a variety of frameworks for selecting interventions when working with a client. The choices are usually made on the basis of some 'objective' diagnosis of the client system, made by client or consultant or both. The difficulties are that, at best, no diagnosis can be complete, and the organisational situation can also change rapidly.

Often both client and consultant are liable to mis-diagnose the particular problem by focusing on the 'reality' of the situation. This creates interventions which attempt to deal with symptoms; result in a ritualistic, cosmetic change, or proposals which gathers dust on somebody's shelf; or are impossible to implement because of resistance (as defined by the consultant and/or project manager).

A Diagnostic Framework

We suggest that considering and interpreting the client's *subjective* psychological reality of the problem offers a useful guide to intervention design. We propose that the presenting problem can offer the opportunity to categorise the client's experience as primarily a sense of:

- *danger* (we feel threatened by this situation)
- *confusion* (we need help to sort this out)
- *conflict* (help us to resolve this conflict)
- *deficit* (give us x, y or z which we need)

When we think about an organisation (or any part of an organisation) as a system, this framework suggests that any disturbance can be classified in at least these four major ways. The framework provides a way of thinking about the organisational system which enables the client and the consultant jointly to explore, contract and evaluate interventions. The categories represent a sequence which can maximise effectiveness in making organisational interventions.

Danger

Where the system is in perceived danger, the staff are either openly panicky and frightened or they are showing many other signs of survival fear such as bravado, over-drinking, unwise risk-taking, loss of creativity and innovation, rigidity and bureaucratisation or engaging in manic over-busyness. This may create an impression of great activity which does not fit with measurable productivity. There can be little quality attention to growth or creativity when many staff members, some key people or the company itself is in severe danger.

When management consultancy is brought in for any other reason than to deal with this perceived danger or to develop plans, strategies and resources to cope with it, avoid it or transform it, the effort will probably be wasted.

If safety is endangered there is little energy left for anything but defensive behaviour. Human biological needs, whether we like it or not, usually take priority. An army cannot march on an empty belly and, no matter how they go through the motions, staff who fear being made redundant will not do their best in developing long-term aims except of course in unusual circumstances. A training programme in strategic long-term management for a group of executives under threat is often ineffective and non-productive. Of course there are always some people for whom a crisis may act as a spur for achievement, but such an effect deteriorates over long-term performance.

However, for taking a company into a new way of working, thinking or behaving well (significant culture change), it is necessary to acknowledge the existence of the danger. This advice may sound obvious but it is in fact rarely implemented. Workers have said; 'We feel crazy when they ask us to make five-year plans and I don't know whether I have a job next month'.

Whether organisational problems are presented as

- *confusion*('help us sort this out')
- *conflict* ('help us resolve this conflict') or
- *deficit* ('give us x, y or z which we need')

it is vital to separate out *danger* issues and deal with them first.

When an organisation is in danger it is important to listen, to acknowledge the feelings, to explore the sources of the danger, assess their reality and deal with the nature of the danger as well as the potential for retrieving or developing resources to deal with it. There may be a temptation to teach when the people are not ready to learn, or to reassure when such reassurance would be false. An organisation or client may also attempt to draw the consultant into 'rescuing' them – taking their responsibility away from them rather than enabling them to deal with the threats to their professional and/or organisational survival in a realistic way.

Confusion

An organisation or team suffering primarily from confusion has difficulty identifying their priorities. They may even have difficulty identifying the problem. They do not know what information is relevant. Prejudices about the company's past performance or management styles are not examined or tested. In the confused organisation, feelings are presented as facts. For example, a manager may be convinced that 'this will not work' instead of a sincere willingness to find out whether 'it may work' and to give the other person, the new policy or the improved machinery the benefit of the doubt. The consultant will notice these and many other signs of confusion.

When a company is unclear about what its business is, when staff are confused about their goals, when there is a general sense of disorientation and lack of direction it is obviously not a good time to deal with conflict or to provide services or resources. Often some parts of management feel that the organisation wants or needs this. The consultant's task is to restrain premature action, and to help to clarify organisational issues, roles and role relationships, authority issues. It is also important to provide models and maps to facilitate exploration of options and choices, and consequent assessment of impact of possible alternative actions.

Engaging in conflict resolution when the individuals, teams or merging companies are unclear about the nature, consequences and significance of conflict is also a waste of time. It is vital that the consultant finds some way of dealing with any danger experienced by the stakeholders first. He or she may then engage with clarifying confusion – without getting drawn into premature attempts to resolve conflict (this is bound to fail), or premature attempts to provide training or development programmes (except those that help people clarify confusion). These are likely to be wasteful and not as effective as if the system had been adequately prepared to receive and use the resources which are provided.

When an organisation (its management or sections of it) is in a confused state it is very important not to get sucked into that confusion. Most consultants have experienced the rapidity and persuasiveness with which they can be drawn into sharing the feeling of confusion and an atmosphere of inability to sort it out which is characteristic of some organisations. At the same time there may be a temptation to oversimplify and reduce the confusion artificially by accepting only one frame of reference, or getting into a fight about the best way forward – thereby creating conflict before the system is ready to deal with it.

Conflict

It is not difficult to diagnose when an organisation, its sections or key individuals are in conflict. This is characterised by clear divisions, a great amount of political activity, categorically different positions, an unwillingness to compromise, and some combination of aggressive shouting matches, or a sullen lack of cooperation which is blatantly hostile but very difficult to pinpoint except as an 'attitude problem'.

If the consultant and the participants are satisfied that there is no real danger in exploring, clarifying or engaging with the conflict, it is possible to begin to use it. Then conflict can become a source of enhanced creativity; anger, aggression and difference can enable everybody in the workplace more effectively and creatively. There used to be a myth that top management teams perform better when they are not in conflict. We know from more recent developments that the existence – even the celebration – of conflict is a profound spur to creativity, innovation and resilience. There are many well- and lesser-known ways of conflict management, conflict resolution or even conflict enhancement. However, as we have pointed out, this is only likely to happen if

- there is no experience *of danger*; for example, if there are no damaging consequences of expressing and standing up for different views
- if the system is not experiencing *confusion*; for example, if there is not widespread vagueness or incapacitating bewilderment about exactly what the issues are.

It may be important for the consultant to learn the history of the conflict in order to discover for example whether it is primarily a personality clash or whether the protagonists (individuals or departments) are interested in common values and the productive outcome to the benefit of all. To gain from the benefits of conflict it is important that the consultant models effective conflict handling – he welcomes it, tries to understand it and works towards resolution. The consultant can become a model and help others to understand conflict and even coach them in better use of aggressive and competitive elements of behaviour. Managers often need to learn or improve their abilities to conflict with others or to manage conflict between others. Providing an arena and referee for the conflict to be acted out – the space, the time and the safety in which to pursue difference and to work towards integrating or co-existence – may also be valuable learning experience.

It is a common consultant error to pathologise conflict – to make people who are in conflict or conflictful feel sick or wrong. This often arises from the consultant's own fear of his or her own aggression or competitiveness. Ignoring or minimising it reduces the possibility for learning from it and benefiting from the potential for enhanced creativity and better understanding which conflict brings in its way. It is obviously not a good idea to take sides unless there is scapegoating where it is necessary to step in.

In creative work environments differences can be valued and quality improved when all parties in a conflict are validated and affirmed. Effective conflict handling promotes and enhances learning and creativity.

Deficit

In this instance an organisation can primarily be characterised as needing something – being in 'deficit'. If it is a new accounting system that the organisation needs, the provision of such system will tend to be satisfying, satisfactory and comparatively easily accomplished. *Training or consultancy which is provided to staff when the deficit is appropriately and accurately identified results in appropriate change in performance.*

However, if consultants or other internal or external 'suppliers' are brought in to give the staff or the organisation something (such as communication skills training, new offices, better systems) and the people are experiencing conflict, confusion or a sense of danger, it is more than likely that the anticipated outcome will not materialise and unpleasant disillusionment and cynical responses are to be expected. On one occasion a request for a management development programme for a specific group of managers (apparently meeting a need) coincided with a move toward downsizing. In this context the client organisation may have been coming from a position of confusion, or the request may have been an attempt to deal with conflict about which of the designated group of managers were to lose their jobs. It is likely that the prospective participants were experiencing danger, were possibly in conflict with each other while competing for the new jobs, and confused about their own future. Without taking these issues into account in contracting and designing this work, the programme would have been a disaster.

Strategic priorities when meeting a deficit are first to establish what people already have as resources, skills, training, options before providing anything. It is also necessary to find out what worked before and what did not and, most importantly, to identify what went wrong before. This is to ensure that the consultant is not working within one of the three previous areas of danger, confusion or conflict.

When one is as certain as possible that there is actually a deficit need it becomes reasonably simple to follow the classic instructions to start from where the clients are, establish their needs and wants, and to provide and review their use of relevant input. A common mistake within this phase is to assume that there is a training solution. Even experienced consultants and trainers have been tempted to provide training or development, customising and implementing their favourite package; only to discover that the recipients of their intervention did not share their understanding of the situation. The intervention may have resulted in a change in behaviour, but not the desired improved performance, because the intervention did not address the problems as experienced by the participants. Another common mistake is to 'do it' for people rather than enabling participants to find, use or discover their own resources.

Application

Using this framework for using the subjective, feeling reality of the client system results in three sets of issues for consultants:

- accurately diagnosing the client's felt need as presented
- understanding that the presenting problem may be only an acceptable way of requesting help on a different underlying issue which the client may or may not be aware of
- choosing an appropriate intervention or intervention strategy aligned to the psychological reality of the situation.

Accurate diagnosis relies on sensitive and accurate perception of relationships within the client system. This develops as the consultant responds to the needs he or she perceives in the client, or experiences the client as having – this provides an initial diagnosis.

However, the communication between client and consultant happens on both conscious and unconscious levels, as illustrated in the following example.

We were approached by a head of a department which provides an advisory service to managers of the company to provide her staff with consultancy skill development. She appeared very clear about what was needed and her request made sense within the context of the company developing a service orientation to its external and internal customers. As we began to work we experienced an unusual amount of difficulty in designing an appropriate programme, and our confusion about what to do increased as we discussed aspects of the proposed programme with the client.

We were tempted to get out of this frustrating situation by blaming the client, cutting our meetings short and just designing something that would 'do'. However, our hunch was that the feeling of confusion we experienced was a response to a part of the (unconscious) communication from the client system – perhaps their own experience of confusion. To make sense of our experience we explored with the client what was going on in the wider organisation. Our diagnostic hunch was confirmed when we were told that a recently-appointed chief executive was expected to introduce large-scale organisational changes. These would have a significant impact on the task of the advisory department. The specifics of the changes were not known, gossip and rumours were rife, and there was a sense of excitement among staff about their involvement in the changes to be introduced. This suggested that the department was experiencing *confusion* and that *danger* was not an issue here. This more thorough understanding then enabled us to design an intervention which addressed the understandable confusion in the system and provided the skill deficit.

Using the consultant's own feelings as guide

Sensitivity to and interpretation of the consultant's own experience while working in the client system offers an opportunity to use both conscious and unconscious communication for richer diagnostic data and thus to confirm or eliminate an initial diagnosis. This experience will be based, at least partially on countertransference – the feelings and thoughts generated in the consultant by fully experiencing the client system (see Table 5.1).

Once these feelings are understood, the consultant can intervene from his full understanding of the client situation. Much less helpfully or possibly dangerously, the consultant may alternatively act from his countertransference (De Board, 1978) without thinking through the meaning of his experience. Using our own and the client's feelings as data about the organisational system can guide us in helping them more effectively.

Table 5.1 Interventions

	Consultant's considered response (countertransference interpreted)	**Consultant's knee-jerk reaction** (countertransference acted out)
Danger	Listen Acknowledge feelings Explore sources Explore nature Elicit emotional reality	Teach falsely Reassure Rescue Contract unrealistically
Confusion	Restrain action Clarify issues Clarify roles Clarify authority Assess impact/consequences Provide models and maps	Get sucked into confusion Oversimplify Accept one frame of reference Fight Take sides
Conflict	Learn its history Welcome and understand it Model conflict handling Value the differences Validate all parties Provide arena and referee	Pathologise it Fear it Minimise it Ignore it Take sides
Deficit	Establish what they have Find what worked before Find out what did not Start where they are Establish needs and wants Provide relevant input	Do it for them Work with solved problems Solve symptoms Give your favourite package Assume there should be a training solution

Conclusion

We have given some practical guidelines on how consultants can use their own feelings in responding to the needs of the client. We distinguish two options for the consultant. The first is the impulsive choice of action because this feels like what the client is really asking for, it is what we know how to do or because of some personal insecurity, chip on the shoulder or favourite hobby-horse. The alternative is to use our own feelings as additional data about the client's system, and allowing these considered feelings to guide us in helping them most efficiently and economically.

Reference

De Board, R. (1978). *The Psychoanalysis of Organisations.* London: Tavistock.

Chapter 6
Human relationships at work in organisations

PETRŪSKA CLARKSON and PATRICIA SHAW

The Problem

Working in organisations is usually not simple. One set of models tries to reduce it to the analysis of parts and their interconnections. Another set of models acknowledge that the relationship between the parts can override any intrinsic relevance of the parts themselves, much as parts of a brain can take over certain functions if the brain is injured in some ways. Even if we accept that all phenomena are relationships, how do we think about and act in regard to changing them?

This is a classification system, imprecise, open-ended, very useful in addressing these questions. It has provided (Clarkson, 1995) the spine for an entire approach to psychotherapy by giving a framework from which any and all of the 450 different approaches to counselling, psychotherapy and psychoanalysis (Corsini, 1986) can be conceptualised, compared and utilised in a coherent, rational and considered way. It might just do the same for consultancy in time.

Introduction

One of the first needs of the human being is for relationship. We know that without it a baby cannot survive, and without it adults cannot thrive (Schaeffer, 1965; Provence and Lipton, 1962). It is to organisational life as water is to a fish. Ever since the Hawthorne experiments of the 1930s (Roethlisberger and Dickson, 1939), organisation theorists and practitioners have recognised that organisations are social systems in which the relationships between people play a vital role. The earlier vision of organisations as efficient, rational machines was undermined by the discovery of the informal, irrational and largely unconscious processes which influence human interaction in the workplace. Ever since, organisations have struggled to understand and meet appropriately the range of human needs at work. As the global environment becomes ever more complex and interdependent, there is a growing recognition of our need to understand further the *patterns* created between people and the implications for organisation functioning.

Another growing trend in organisational life is the attempt to create provision, either directly or through other agencies, for the acquisition of organisational counselling skills. There is a recognition that employees at any level in the organisation may need access to counselling services and also that many employees, such as supervisors, managers, trainers and internal consultants, need to have some counselling skills to work competently with others. For example, managers are routinely expected to contribute ably to the performance appraisal, career progression and personal development of staff. This sometimes leads to a number of confusions. One such is the confusion between managerial and so-called counselling roles with the risk of potential diminishment of effectiveness in both. Another difficulty arises when counselling is seen as providing an increase in psychological knowledge or emotional awareness, which may or may not be accompanied by a cost-effective return in terms of the quality or quantity of work accomplished. A further confusion is born of the recognition that some of the psychological and emotional needs of workers cannot appropriately be met within

Table 6.1 An assessment framework for relationships at work

Relationship	Contribution to the organisation	Human motivation	Some signs of dysfunction
Unfinished	Grit in the oyster	Completion Resolution	Fixed, disruptive patterns of relationship
Working alliance	Achieving organisational tasks	Doing Competence Productivity	Task-dominated culture Sterile, driven work climate
Developmental	Developing the organisation's human resources	Growth Learning	Neediness Burn-out Over- or under-protection of staff
Personal	Developing the organisation as a working community with a healthy culture	Intimacy Friendship Community Loss of task focus	Uncontactful conflict and competition Fake bonhomie
Transpersonal	Developing wider organisation mission and purpose	Being Meaning Connection	Meaninglessness Anomie Ennui Disregard of ethics

the mainstream work of the organisation. This has led to the creation of facilities for counselling services to employees separate from managerial structures, and often confidential. However, when peoples' difficulties concern normal adjustment phases, for example, at promotion or in response to family bereavement, appropriate counselling *at the workplace* is likely to cause minimum disruption of the worker's productivity and, in the long term, may benefit the company by enhancing the wellbeing and morale of staff. Organisations need help in understanding when and how counselling which aims to improve relationship functioning, can be directly related to task performance.

To help clarify the roles of counselling and consulting skills and services within a healthy organisation, we will differentiate between five aspects of relationship at work:

- the *unfinished relationship*
- the *working alliance*
- the *developmental relationship*
- the *personal relationship*
- the *transpersonal relationship*.

We hypothesise that all human beings need all of these relationships in varying degrees and at different stages in their lives, and that the human need for these relationships is, after physiological survival, the primary motivation of the person. As these are continuing adult needs, we believe that a healthy organisation is probably one that supports people in developing all five kinds of relationship within its overall fabric.

These ideas also provide another basis for understanding human motivation in organisational life.

- The *unfinished relationship* carries the human need for healing from the conflicts and hurts of the past.
- The *working alliance* satisfies our need for doing and for competence.
- The *developmental relationship* carries our deficits and our need for growth.
- The *personal relationship* carries our self needs, our need for recognition as unique individuals.
- The *transpersonal relationship* carries our need for being, meaning and connection.

Table 6.1 summarises the five relationships in terms of their contribution to the organisation, the ways in which they may be dysfunctional, and the human motivation needs that each can satisfy.

The first segment of the table is meant for the contribution of the unfinished relationship to an organisation. At this point, we cannot see any real value for this relationship, unless we consider that the exploitation of people's neurotic or even pathological patterns in the service of organisational goals can be justified. This strikes us as an interesting and controversial area. Is it useful or even possible to distinguish between people choosing careers or types of organisations in order to exercise their talents, from those situations where the choice of work is in fact a collusive one which prevents people from facing unresolved issues in their lives? For example, when is a manager's drive for executive power a desire to contribute to the organisation in a leadership role, and when could it be, perhaps, destructively perfectionistic or deriving from an unhealthy need for control, or status? However, perhaps this can be the grit in the oyster of organisational life if it is used constructively.

We will now describe the true aspects of human relationship at work in more detail.

The Unfinished Relationship

This is the relationship which can get in the way of *all* the others. It is sometimes referred to as the transferential or projected relationship, because the person 'transfers' or 'projects' elements of other, past relationships into this present one. It is characterised by unrealistic hopes or fears, loyalties or resentments which may or may not correspond with the actualities of the individual's current work situation. This is when peoples' reactions are inappropriate, exaggerated, overly defensive, and sometimes destructive of the contractual working relationship.

For example, the contract between the organisation and the worker may require punctual time-keeping. When a worker repeatedly violates this contract for little apparent reason, even though he or she really needs to keep the job, the supervisor may be puzzled by the contradiction between the worker's stated intention to improve the attendance and the apparent inability or unwillingness to actually do so. Even while the worker in some way understands and agrees the contract, another part of them feels the boss is being unreasonable in not accepting another good excuse. Another example could be the case of a manager who may want, and in fact receives, repeated reassurance that he or she is doing good work, but this makes little difference to the person's insecurity and low self-esteem, which continue to detract from an otherwise effective performance.

In many of these cases historical expectations of parental punishment, or childish wishes for protection or appreciation which were not gratified in the person's childhood, interfere with the capacity to make appropriate working relationships or to sustain these under stress. It is not the organisation's task to provide staff with the love and security which they deserved to have from their parents as children. However, organisations do need to deal with the fact that projection or transference, whether in subtle or extreme forms, is the source of much misunderstanding, disappointment and lack of productivity in the workplace. Experiments in gestalt psychology suggest that everyone, to a greater or lesser extent, carries the need to finish or complete unresolved situations from their personal history. (Perls *et al.,*1969). Entering into present relationships based on projection from the past is an important way in which people strive to meet this need. It is potentially (but not certainly) growthful for them as individuals to do this, however dysfunctional it may be for the organisation.

There are a number of ways in which organisations can begin to deal with this situation. Perhaps the most important is good-humoured acceptance of unfinished relationships as a fact of life. Renn Zaphiropoulos, when president of Versatec, one of the worlds largest producers of electrostatic printers, was wont to include in his induction talk to new employees, the exhortation 'Please remember at all times that your boss is *not* your mother or your father!' (Kotter, 1980). Once the existence of unfinished relationships at work, however undesirable, is acknowledged, people can learn, first to recognise them and distinguish them from other kinds of relationship, and then to develop the skills to minimise, neutralise, or channel the energies of the unfinished relationship back into the here-and-now task. In our experience, this is a key underdeveloped competence in organisations. It is not to be confused with entry into the unfinished relationship for the purpose of transforming it into opportunities for positive growth, for which extensive psychotherapeutic training and skill may be required. This is an area which managers can find very confusing, as they repeatedly attempt to deal with the symptoms of the unfinished relationship without addressing its cause.

Where a situation seems particularly intractable, involving fixed, compulsively re-enacted patterns of relationship between an employee and one figure of authority after another, organisations can use qualified counsellors or psychotherapists. These are people who are skilled and specifically trained in using the projections therapeutically by helping people to 'finish the unfinished business' which is still interfering with their current lives and work. Such professionals have undergone their own personal counselling or psychotherapy in order to ensure they do not enter unwisely or ignorantly into complementary (countertransferential) situations beyond their competence.

We believe it is preferable for counselling services, including a professional referral service, to be a permanent facility within the organisation, rather than something provided as an *ad hoc* response to crises. Only in this way can opportunities to enter into unfinished relationships productively be part of the overall fabric of the organisation. Companies may need to realise that normal competent people with skills and abilities of value to the organisation may benefit from this kind of help at some time during their working lives, particularly in order to handle well the issues of dependence, authority and power which are an inevitable part of organisations.

The focus on unfinished *relationships,* rather than solely on the difficulties of individuals, points to the possibility of counselling provision for significant working partnerships of two or more people where mutual projection of historical issues is trapping all parties into a dysfunctional pattern, which drains energy from organisationally useful activity. Indeed this is often an important aspect of effective teamwork consultancy. Again, this is not to be confused with third-party mediation within or between working groups where mutual assumptions and stereotyping are the results of poor communication *in the present.* It is perfectly appropriate that managers, as well as trainers and internal facilitators, should develop the skills to work effectively with these latter kinds of situations, while distinguishing them from cases of symbiotic, unfinished relationships for which external, more qualified help may be needed.

As soon as we move away from support to the individual employee, organisations are likely to be using the term *consulting* rather than *counselling*, although in the sense that we are using the terms, both are services in the support of effective relationship functioning.

The Working Alliance

This is the relationship between two or more people which is constructed around a shared task, whether that be the flotation of a public company or bringing up children together. This is the kind of relationship which is most desired in organisations and frequently least achieved despite the fact that it is natural for people to want to complete satisfactorily the tasks and activities in which they are engaged. If human beings were rational, logical, and always acted in their own best interests, working alliance relationships would be the norm. When the working relationship is sound and effective the work of the group or the task of the organisation gets done with the minimum of interference or delay. When it is interrupted or dysfunctional one can frequently hear frustrated cries of: 'Why can't we just get on with it!' This happens when people do not know how to recognise manifestations of the unfinished relationship which may be introducing irrational, unconscious factors that sabotage the alliance.

At its best, the healthy working alliance is characterised by love of the work and the satisfaction of working with others in a task which has personal meaning for all those involved, as well as a collective ownership of the project. It is both *my* task and *our* task. Energy for the work comes from within the partners in the alliance and supports the organisation instead of needing to be driven or supported by it. This kind of relationship is to be found in good project teams and task forces, which may appear to others as groups of exuberant and celebratory workaholics.

From a counselling point of view, the key here lies in helping people to discover and act on their true wants and talents in relation to work. Career-related counselling may be valuable at many stages in a person's working life: not only at the start, but for the plateaued manager, or for the employee facing early retirement. Good job plans, goal-setting and performance appraisal in which employee and manager work together to structure assignments which maximise the possibility for achievement, productivity and expression of competence is one way in which organisations can energise the natural capacity of human beings to work hard on tasks they really want to do.

Effective working alliance relationships become more and more important as organisations move away from bureaucratic control towards matrix structures, project teams and organic networks. There has been a tendency in the last twenty years to focus on interpersonal issues for team-building purposes at the expense of developing the skills of *working* together productively. This arises from the confusion between the needs of the working alliance, the unfinished relationship and the personal relationship. It is noticeable that the most effective working alliances need fewer process and review meetings!

A distorted and dysfunctional form of the working alliance can be found in organisations which expect working on tasks to fulfil all the human needs in the organisation. People may work hard together but there is a certain grimness and sterility about the undertaking. The working relationships are functioning to lock people together, each as the gaoler of the other and all as prisoners of the task. Spontaneity and joy in the work are absent. Although some hard-pressed managers may not see either of these as primary goals at work, they are essential for creativity. When they are lacking, the productivity of those involved has to be driven by external energy in the form of tight supervision, managerial controls, or purely financial reward systems. The managerial energy expended in order to maintain high task performance in this way is often not taken into account.

The Developmental Relationship

It is important to distinguish this relationship from the unfinished one. The focus here is on developing the *adult* professional, not undertaking to make up to the employee for the deficiencies of his or her parents, caretakers, or educators. This means providing an individual with the information, support and challenge which they need now to meet their development needs. These will vary depending on the tasks, the stage of career progression, the level of maturity and the idiosyncrasies of the individual. One of the major requirements for a developmental relationship is empathic attunement to the potential for growth of the individual, taking into account the critical phases at which people are most ready to learn new skills or attitudes. This does not mean solving the individual's problems for them but providing them with the kinds of relationship qualities which empower the individual to take appropriate levels of responsibility in discovering how to develop themselves.

There has been increasing recognition in recent years that counselling skills in this particular sense are an essential component of managerial competence in addition to the task performance appraisal of staff. Many managers now receive training in coaching, counselling and enabling skills, so that they can undertake both the development and the appraisal of staff. Some organisations have experimented with appointing mentors who deliberately have no line responsibility for the individual being developed, but actively participate in the professional development of the, usually, junior colleague. We imagine, although it is rarely articulated in this way, that the boss/subordinate relationship is the one most likely to trigger the projected elements of the unfinished relationship, which may sabotage the possibility of an effective developmental relationship. Unfortunately, separating mentor and boss could succeed in reinforcing this, because the line manager may be seen as the disciplinarian, and the mentor the fairy godmother. What is really needed is that managers are sufficiently skilled and informed to create and sustain the developmental relationship without unnecessarily eliciting or encouraging the unfinished one.

A healthy form of the developmental relationship is characterised by being based on explicit, consciously-chosen, contractual agreements between the parties involved which spell out their mutual responsibilities. What is exchanged in the relationship will necessarily change over time because adults continue to develop and evolve over their entire life span. In contrast, the projected relationship is based on unconscious expectations, no explicit contractual agreements, and remains fixed and repetitive in nature. Good developmental relationships can be therapeutic for individuals by providing productive, affirming experiences in the present. For example, good training experiences may be therapeutic in giving employees experiences of learning situations where they are treated as competent, curious learners without threat of physical or verbal abuse, which may be immensely repairing of poor early schooling. The difference between a 'transferential' and a 'developmental' relationship is that, in the latter, the person is left empowered, more autonomous and better resourced for the future, rather than negatively dependent.

An apparent developmental relationship, which is in fact not supporting the growth of the individual, is one in which employees are not helped to discriminate between their aspirations and their capacities, or where they are catapulted into premature assumption of responsibilities without sufficient support or preparation. This can lead to a pseudo-competency syndrome which is characterised by objective assessments of competence but subjective experiences of incompetence, uncertainty and precariously snatched successes (see Chapter 8). Although it is important for providers of this relationship to be involved with the people whom they are mentoring, it is counterproductive if they are vicariously drawn into the issues. An inordinate or inappropriate investment in the other person's success or failure can be very detrimental and damaging. A certain objectivity makes for clearer vision, unlike the personal relationship.

The Personal Relationship

This relationship is based on subjective appreciation of another. It involves trust and authenticity, as do all healthy organisational relationships to varying degrees. However, this does not imply a situation of unconditional trust. It does mean affirmation and respect of a person's intrinsic self-worth, but does not imply unconditional acceptance of behaviour which may be disruptive or unproductive. Shared tasks, shared experiences and shared values often lead to feelings of closeness, affection and intimacy among colleagues in the workplace. This is very understandable and human, and is a significant part of why people work. The social pleasures, emotional stimulation and sense of community which can be achieved in the healthy workplace is vital to the accomplishment of the task. It is also not surprising that many people meet their life partners at work.

Companies may build upon the personal relationship to support organisational purposes when they set up self-development groups or in-company action learning sets during company time. Here people can develop their ability to offer one another collegial authenticity, sharing without burdening, and listening without caretaking. The competencies needed are interpersonal and contact skills.

When personal relationships are so strong that they become more important than the organisational task, they become dysfunctional for the individuals and the organisation. For example, inappropriate friendships, sexual relationships, joint financial or leisure projects may in some way compromise the resources of the firm, whether in time, energy or materials. Whether personal relationships contribute to and enhance the organisation's cultural well-being depends on how people respond to organisational demands. If it is with resentment, as in the obvious example of shop assistants chatting behind the counter who do their best to ignore a prospective customer, then it is organisationally dysfunctional.

Personal relationships between boss and subordinate are often open to difficulty because the boss retains the capacity to hire and fire and to reward or deny. This may lead to a sense of betrayal in the subordinate and to painful conflict for the boss which may impair his or her decision-making in cases of 'downsizing' or promotion, for example. Only a high degree of trust and honesty, as well as a strong sense of personal security in both people, can make this relationship really work.

Another way in which personal relationships may have negative consequences occurs when in reality these relationships are weak but appearances make them out to be strong. This applies to the organisational hard-drinking fraternity, the ritual Christmas office party, the hail-fellow-well-met sales conference. All of these may give the appearance of intimacy without the substance. Any major organisational change (restructuring, for example) quickly reveals fear, distrust and self-serving behaviour, which it is very difficult to face and work through openly.

The Transpersonal Relationship

The transpersonal relationship is here used to denote a sense of connection between individuals or groups which is deeper than the relationships we have so far discussed, and extends beyond the people that any one individual knows or works with. Different people may have different conceptions of this dimension of human and organisational experience. We are talking here about the transpersonal relationship *between people* and not only that between the individual and his or her personal god or however they may construe ultimate values. The most concrete form in which this has become acceptable in organisations is the growing preoccupation with organisational cultures, mission statements, organisational vision and values. These are all ways in which connections between people create something more than the sum of their individual selves. Increasingly organisations are incorporating these into written statements, slogans or even lengthy brochures. However, leaders in organisations often fail to distinguish between what can and cannot be achieved by such collective statements. In particular, a vision or a sense of mission is confused with a product rather than a living process. The board of directors who formulated the vision or mission statement may well have shared some sense of transpersonal relationship. This will not necessarily be recreated in the delivering of the product to others in the organisation.

To develop transpersonal relationships people need to appreciate the profound connectivity and interdependence of human beings to one another, nature, and even the universe. Until recently our science, philosophy and psychology have emphasised separateness. So far, organisations too have concentrated on the separation and subsequent linking of roles, tasks and responsibilities in a very analytic, left-hemispheric and digital approach. We have taught people segments and now we need them to create organisational wholes, but the complexity of the interacting variables has exceeded the well-worn analytical methods. There is a growing recognition (sometimes born of despair) among workers and academics that new paradigms need to be made. Modern science is now providing us with such paradigms. Many disciplines: chaos theory (Gleick, 1987) quantum physics (Bohm, 1980) and Lovelock's Gaia hypothesis (1988), which suggests that our planet is one living organism, all offer examples which can only be understood through the principle of connectivity. Gestalt psychology since the 1930s has been concerned with a holistic approach, particularly the human need to create meaningful wholes from all our experiences and perceptions (Koffka, 1935; Kohler, 1970; Wertheimer, 1944). These ideas, though they can only be most briefly indicated in a chapter of this length, provide a source of education for transpersonal leadership at all levels of an organisation.

Organisational leaders such as Richard Branson or Anita Roddick, and social leaders such as Bob Geldof, suggest the kind of qualities and relationships that draw groups of people into achievement of sometimes extraordinary vision. It is noticeable that these are leaders who created organisations that achieved financial viability as well as being environmentally responsible. The genuinely transpersonal leader or teacher enables people to find their own sources of meaning and purpose within themselves, and facilitates modes of expression for the collective. Such a person enables the flowering of shared wants and values which are organismic, natural and exist independently of the leader.

Organisations which pay no attention to the transpersonal are those without heart or spirit, that just go through the motions. Some City financial institutions in the 1980s became places of aridity and meaninglessness for those who worked in them, with career burn-out occurring at a very early age. Less severe forms of the same malaise may be found in the low morale of manufacturing industries which still rely entirely upon the production line model, and in the more stifling forms of clerical bureaucracy, where people do not have a sense of making a difference to the world, and absenteeism and errors are rife.

Implications for Counselling and Consulting Skills and Services

We have suggested here five aspects of relationship 'at work' in organisations. We can now see how many of the training needs which are commonly identified in organisations are linked to these different aspects. Table 6.2 suggests the key skills needed by those involved in each type of relationship. We believe that this framework may enable a more finely-tuned diagnosis and design for relationship training and process consultancy in organisations.

People need to develop the ability to recognise the five different kinds of relationship, to distinguish them from one another, and to decide on the appropriateness of each one in a given situation. In meeting such training needs, an organisation needs to judge when to use internal resources or to engage external help. We would suggest that working with the unfinished relationship often requires skills and experience less likely to be found in many organisations, although we believe it is very important that internal trainers, facilitators and consultants appreciate the nature of this relationship, the skills needed to work with it, and the extent of their own competence. In our experience, the importance of this aspect of working relationships needs to be much better appreciated in organisations. For example, the current emphasis on creating empowerment in organisations through greater involvement and shared responsibility for decisions and actions at all levels is sometimes bedevilled by problems which have at their root people's unresolved difficulties with issues of dependence, self-responsibility and personal change.

Table 6.2 Assessment framework for supporting human relationships at work

Relationship	Relationship skills training	Counselling and consulting services
Unfinished	Capacity to recognise, minimise, neutralise, rechannel energy from unfinished relationship issues into the here-and-now task Developing self-awareness Dealing with 'games-playing'	Qualified psychotherapy and counselling for individuals, groups and the organisation as a whole
Working alliance	Productive work cycle skills Team working skills Project team leading skills	Team consultancy Occupational assessment
Developmental	Teaching, coaching, counselling and enabling skills Mentoring and modelling skills	Career development counselling Training and development experiences
Personal	Interpersonal skills Emotional fluency Contactful communication Skills in managing personal boundaries Sensitivity training Group process skills	Personal counselling Employee assistance Affective education
Transpersonal	Skills in catalysing meaningful wholes for a collective, e.g. shared vision, mission, values Leadership development	Whole organisation counselling, e.g. organisational development consultancy

References

Bohm, D. (1980). *Wholeness and the Implicate Order.* London: Ark.
Clarkson, P. (1995). *The Therapeutic Relationship.* London: Whurr.
Corsini, R. (ed.) (1986). *Current Psychotherapies.* Illinois: F.E. Peacock.
Gleick, J. (1987). *Chaos: Making a New Science.* London: Heinemann.
Koffka, K. (1935). *Principles of Gestalt Psychology.* New York: Harcourt, Brace and World.
Kohler, W. (1970). *Gestalt Psychology. An Introduction to New Concepts in Modern Psychology.* New York: Liverights (first published 1947).
Kotter, J. P. (1980). *Renn Zaphiropoulos.* HBS Case Services, Harvard Business School.
Lovelock, J. (1988). *The Ages of Gaia.* Oxford: Oxford University Press.
Provence, S., and Lipton, R. C. (1962). *Infants in Institutions.* New York: International Universities Press.
Perls, F. S., Hefferline, R. F. and Goodman, P. (1969). *Gestalt Therapy: Excitement and Growth in the Human Personality.* New York: Julian Press (first published 1951).
Roethlisberger, F. J. and Dickson, W. J. (1939). *Management and the Worker.* Cambridge, MA: Harvard University Press.
Schaeffer, H. R. (1965). 'Change in developmental quotient under two conditions of maternal separation', *British Journal of Social Clinical Psychology.* 4, 39–46.
Wertheimer, M. (1944). 'Gestalt Theory', *Social Research* II(i), 78–99.

Chapter 7
Professional development, personal development and counselling and psychotherapy

How to differentiate and negotiate boundaries in organisational work

PETRŪSKA CLARKSON and SUSAN CLAYTON

The Problem

Organisational consultants, supervisors, trainers, even managers are always asking: where is the line between counselling and consultancy, personal development and professional development, individual work and team process, and so on and so forth. It is one of the most frequently recurring questions in the field. The more practitioners know about counselling and psychotherapy, the worse it sometimes gets. And just because they know more, it does not mean that the problems left or create by practitioners rushing in where angels fear to tread are any less destructive, handicapping or damaging. Of course there is no line as such, and yet again there is.

Introduction

The purpose of this chapter is to raise the awareness of the diversity between professional development, personal development and counselling or psychotherapy when working in organisations. An identifiable boundary between the three can enable the consultant and group leader to facilitate learning through more clearly focused interventions. As Harrison (1983, p. 224) states 'It is by labelling that we create meanings'. Through meaning we create values and can then act consistently according to them. 'It is in the creation of valued meaning that leadership focuses and channels human energy'. Thus through this chapter we hope to create meaning for those working as trainers, course facilitators and consultants as well as managers and supervisors who want to under-

Professional and personal development

stand these boundaries more fully. We can then identify ways of working more powerfully with learning groups.

The problem we address arises because the interpretation of 'personal development' encompasses many areas of growth, ranging from technical skills in a chosen profession through to counselling and intensive psychotherapy. For this purpose we will identify personal development as the overlap between professional development and counselling or psychotherapy, as illustrated in Fig. 7.1. This diagram also symbolises the mandorla (from medieval theology). With similar healing properties to the mandala (a Sanskrit term from India and Tibet), which is a circle representing wholeness, the mandorla is the almond shape created by two partly overlapping circles. The symbol signifies the overlapping of opposites, the healing and integration of split parts of the self. Initially the overlap is small, but as a person continues to develop so the overlap increases and they become more whole (Johnson, 1991). Here personal development is the mandorla, it is the integration of the doing self and the being self in such a way that creates wholeness. Frequently these two parts of the self become split in the working environment.

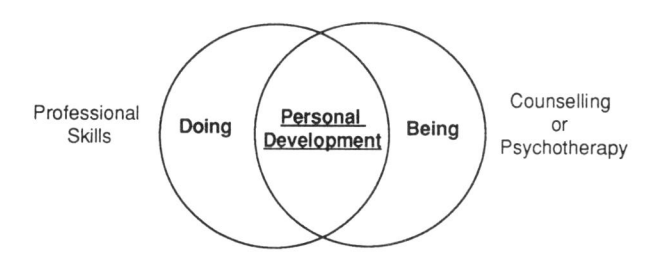

Figure 7.1 The overlap between professional development and counselling or psychotherapy.

People come into learning or development from different motivations, they choose a profession because it suits their style. For example a dyslexic student chooses teaching PE as their profession to avoid struggling with the effects of their disability in reading and writing; computer technologists develop highly sophisticated skills communicating with a computer but their abilities to communicate with people may be inadequate for the industry when they are solitary people. This latter example is common in the IT industry where often technologists do not communicate well interpersonally; their preference is to work in relative isolation with the computer. Yet there arises from this a conflict in needs. Organisationally, good quality interpersonal communication is essential for success. Effective groupwork is the key to this, but the individual need is to work in relative isolation. The problem then becomes amplified when the technologist takes on a managerial role in which working well with others is essential to successful management. Developing communication skills may help in the short term, but combined with personal development would enable individuals to understand themselves more fully. It would also be more likely to achieve long-term and wider benefits for themselves and the organisation.

Doing (Professional Development)

In this model our description of professional development is the transfer of knowledge skills and techniques which are instrumental – the essential information and skills required for a chosen profession, learning how to do, doing. Whether it is learning the skills of carpentry, where the carpenter learns how to give shape and form to wood for a specific purpose; accounting, when a person is taught how to audit and prepare business accounts and reports in tax and finance; the artist, who develops skills to express their creativity through painting, drawing, sculpture; psychotherapy, where the therapist, through practice and theoretical understanding, learns how to treat mental pain by therapeutic communication; or the executive skills of business management, where a person develops the skills and knowledge to manage both people and specific aspects of running a business (i.e. marketing, sales, finance, productivity, human resources).

These skills are developed through the education system, higher education, training, supervision, coaching and mentoring, the latter two being problem-solving and advisory roles. Training is achieved by passing on information through tutoring, lectures and 'classroom' format, developing skill competence through practise and supervision.

The doing person will seek achievement, recognition power, status and competency. There are many, many professional people, managers, executives who do little to develop themselves personally, only professionally and are successful due to their charisma, drive for success and power, or authoritarian nature or natural autonomy.

Being (Counselling and Psychotherapy)

The being circle represents the personal and private self, where both counselling and personal therapy enables the development process of learning how to become and be oneself more fully in the world. This process can range from a single counselling session to long-term psychotherapy. These two disciplines are often confused as there is considerable overlap between them. To help your understanding we will briefly describe their differences. These descriptions have been drawn from (Clarkson 1991, 1994) where a more comprehensive comparison is given.

In comparing psychotherapy with counselling Clarkson (1991) states that

> Counselling assists people in finding the solution to a particular problem or dealing with a particular crisis, whereas usually psychotherapy helps people to develop new ways of solving problems which can become generalised to new situations. (p. 11)

She goes on to say that counselling deals mostly with current situations, in contrast to psychotherapy which deals with the past, although there are many exceptions to this description.

Counselling:

> The overall aim is to provide an opportunity to work towards living more satisfyingly and resourcefully. Counselling relationships will vary according to need but may be concerned with developmental issues, addressing and resolving specific problems, making decisions, coping with crisis, developing personal insights and knowledge, working through feelings of inner conflict, or improving relationships with others. (BAC, 1989, p.1).

Counselling at work is a specialised field requiring specific counselling skills and knowledge of organisational functioning. A counselling facility in an organisation may consist of an on-site counsellor and in the bought-in services of external consultants for executing counselling. Redundancy counselling is typical of this process, others are stress counselling, retirement counselling, health counselling and career counselling, which many organisations offer as a free service to their employees. Clarkson (1994) states that 'counsellors at work help to oil the wheels of someone's experience so that they manage to function better'.

Counselling will provide support and encourage personal growth through issues such as life events, work difficulties and organisational change. With adequate training, managers can also use counselling skills with their teams to engender good communications, improve performance and increase personal effectiveness within the department and the organisation. This way counselling is used pro-actively rather than only being available for reparatory work.

The normal process of counselling is to assist people in finding the solution to a particular problem, to deal with a particular crisis, generally of a current situation and explore ways of living life more resourcefully. Meetings with the counsellor are at regular intervals over a short period of time. Counselling tends to focus on evolutionary change, which uses existing behaviour to achieve a particular outcome. It usually does not attempt to create fundamental change to core behaviour patterns.

Psychotherapy

In contrast to counselling, psychotherapy will tend to deal more with

...ations, helping clients to find new ways of solving problems ...an then become generalised to new situations. Psychotherapy is ...nally seen as healing the sick but increasingly recognised as a tool for personal growth and self understanding: it is a process of heightening awareness and changing behaviour. Zinker (1977, p. 121) refers to two types of therapy which work at two different levels. He argues that 'most therapies are designed to cure common pathologies resulting from frustration of lower level needs', like love, belonging, recognition, achievements and competencies. He compares this to meta needs and meta sicknesses where therapy deals with the deepest levels of human needs caused by sicknesses in society or spiritual suffering. Most therapies are designed to work with the first of these two levels. This is where therapy and personal development become so entangled, as that is also the region where excitement and energy exists for personal development.

Clarkson (1994) views the psychotherapeutic relationship as active in destructuring and restructuring the personality where the client works on identified repetitive behaviours which are having a negative effect on the client's present life. This frequently entails working with childhood and historic material where the client attends therapy on a regular basis over a long period of time. The aim is revolutionary rather than evolutionary change, where revolutionary change requires a fundamental change of mind or character. This is important when clarifying the boundaries in organisational work and looking at the problems which arise if these boundaries are not clear or maintained.

Therapy is rarely available as a service for employees in organisations, although some mental health institutions will provide therapy groups for their employees as part of a support system to maintain 'psychological fitness' in their work. In this case it is recognised that the job has a particular stress on psychological health, e.g. psychiatric nursing. Issues addressed would tend to focus on those arising through work. Generally speaking those who seek therapy find this outside of work, which is probably most appropriate in view of the nature of psychotherapy and the processes involved.

This is not to say that trainers and course facilitators operating in the working environment have not been exposed to psychotherapy or counselling training. It is often the case that an interest in people leads to studying psychology, training in counselling skills and psychotherapy, and more specialised disciplines such as T-groups, gestalt, transactional analysis, NLP, humanistic psychology, co-counselling, psychodynamic and analytic disciplines. It is this rich and varied field that can, paradoxically, have a detrimental affect on a group member attending a personal development programme. In pursuing knowledge from various disciplines without taking the skills to sufficient depth to handle issues which

Danger of lack of training

may emerge in a group, the facilitator may not have enough skills or knowledge to understand and deal with emerging issues, resulting in psychological damage to the group member. For example, a group member becomes angry at the facilitator. With an interest in, say, gestalt, the facilitator seeks catharsis, unknowingly leading the group member close to a dangerous (psychotic) state; then, believing that good work has been achieved, leaves the person in a state of helplessness, in need of support and ongoing therapy to deal with repressed material brought to the surface too quickly and insensitively.

In management development workshops the temptation to go down the therapy route can, at the least, leave the unsuspecting trainee bewildered and unsure what has happened to them, at the worst devastated with no one to pick them up and help them move on. Therefore where group leaders have skills in this field they should also have very careful training in how to apply these skills in personal development, identifying clear boundaries.

Even when a course appears to have 'succeeded' from the point of view of the course organisers, family and friends are often disturbed by mysterious changes in an individual's personality. Not surprisingly, many psychiatrists are alarmed by the damage such training can do.

The sad fact is that this report probably reflects the experiences of many naive customers of management training programmes where group leaders are working from a position of limited knowledge and experience of psychology and psychotherapy and using this knowledge to manipulate others. One consequence of this is that personal development does not gain recognition for the good work which can be achieved through skilled and sensitive facilitation.

Personal Development

Professional learning, which focuses on *how to do*, and therapeutic learning, which focuses on *how to be,* can actually be regarded as quite separate and diverse aspects of 'gaining information' for the self. From this we hypothesise that when these two parts of the learning self overlap, the doing self and the being self, there emerges an area of potential growth that is fundamentally different in learning than either of the other two. The learning which occurs here is a gestalt, possessing qualities that cannot be described as purely the sum of doing and being combined. This is the learning arena we refer to as *personal development*.

The size of the personal development arena varies according to the amount of personal development which the individual has experienced, not according to the amount of learning which has occurred in either professional development or in therapy, although there may be influences across the boundaries. So one of the characteristics of personal development is that of an integrating effect of these two aspects of the self. The qualities which emerge through personal development might be described as authenticity, integrity, unique style, strong sense of presence, well groundedness, having an ability to separate professional competence from personal characteristics and knowing the influence each has on the other. For example, a company director was highly competent in his specialised area of work in accounting, but not so competent in managing people where he seemed unable to gain respect from his staff. Having had no training in management skills he managed people through a position of authority, as he thought they 'should' be managed, rather than establishing a personal style for himself by integrating his theory of good management (doing) with his own personal style (being). This would have led to a more authentic way of managing, more likely to have gained the respect from his staff that he longed for.

The Difference Between Professional Development Groups and Personal Development Groups

Professional development is essentially the transfer of knowledge, skills and techniques that form the basis of professional advancement. Frequently people progress through a profession simply on the basis of technical competence in the chosen profession, which is traditional in practices such as solicitors and accounting firms.

Simple comparisons between professional and personal development are shown in Table 7.1. We will discuss in more depth the three key differences: the role of the group leader, the leaning process and the amount of struture adopted.

The role of the group leader and the depth of interaction which occurs

Probably thanks to our traditional methods of learning through the education system, there seems to be no problem around what trainees expect from the group leader in professional development, where boundaries are relatively clear. This is not always so in personal development, and it is certainly an area which could be and needs to be more clearly defined. If the leader is unsure what their role is or their boundaries are, then the trainees will be unsure and the potential for learning reduced.

A quite significant difference between these two styles of teaching is

Professional and personal development

Table 7.1 Professional and personal development groups

Professional development groups	Personal development groups
Role of group leader	
Leader is authority figure	Leader is in authority yet has fluid movement within the group
The influence of the leader and 'field' on the group is not a deliberate part of the learning process	Influence of the leader and 'field' on the group and individuals will be used as part of the learning process
Trainers usually work within a specialised area	Leaders are more effective if they have a wide range of knowledge and experience, as well as specialist skills
The learning process	
Transfer of skills and knowledge for the benefit of technical competence	Integration of skills and knowledge, old and new, with personal self
Engages solely with the doing self	Engages with both the doing and being self
General assumption that the transfer of learning will be managed by the trainee	Transfer of learning is usually regarded as a complex and challenging process, often supported through the programme structure
No attempt to engage feelings	Engaging feelings at some stage is fundamental to the process
The structure	
Generally work with highly structured format	Work within a framework but with considerable flexibility according to the group's emerging needs
Large and small formal and informal groups, depending on the skills being developed	Medium and small informal groups

in acknowledging and using the influence of the leader and the environment as part of the learning process. Professional development will occasionally recognise the influence of the leader on the trainees, as opposed to the experienced personal development group leader who acknowledges both the immediate field (i.e. the current environment, group and leader) and the wider field (i.e. the working environment, organisation culture, personal life and history, society, etc.), as influences in the development process. In fact this is essential to generating rich, meaningful insights for personal development.

A further difference is that of dependence. There is a clear dependency on the group leader in professional development to deliver information – that is their role. However, to develop such dependency in personal development work is highly disempowering for group members and dysfunctional for the consultant.

The learning process

There is an implicit assumption in professional development that all people learn in the same way, that the learning material will have the same meaning for everyone, that the application of learning will be straight forward. Trainees often walk away from training with more tools in their kitbag, more ideas and techniques, yet 'remain fundamentally untouched themselves' (Phillips and Shaw 1989, p. 101). For example, a group of cashiers will learn how to handle money and balance their till at the end of the day, all learning the same information at a similar level of competency and assimilating this at roughly the same pace. In contrast, the skilled leader of a personal development group will not assume with 100% certainty the likely outcome of the training for each individual or the group. They will work only on strong probabilities, based on their own influence and interventions. So a communication skills workshop may include some theory. How individuals integrate and apply that theory will depend on a number of things such as their current style of communication, their level of interest in the subject, their personality, their history.

For personal development a good leader will respect different learning styles and discuss the process of transferring what has been learned, to the working environment. This transfer will be regarded as complex and challenging and will inevitably involve a period of uncertainty when learning how to apply new skills (see Chapter 8), going through a period of 'conscious incompetence', with all the risks and difficulties associated with it. This will involve feeling unsure, pretending to be relatively competent at being different and learning through error. Such a process is often well supported where the programme design in-corporates a follow-up to the core training, as in action-learning programmes.

Many personal development programmes will include imparting some knowledge, skills and techniques and exploring new information, in response to the needs of the group. In contrast professional development does not necessarily include personal development.

This difference is stated in a recent study by Boydell *et al.* (1991) where they saw it necessary to differentiate between training (comparable to our use of professional development) and development. They suggest that

... Development may well involve training; but training in itself is not necessarily developmental. That is, training may often be a necessary condition for development, but of itself is not sufficient.

They describe training as 'A relatively systematic attempt to transfer knowledge or skills from one who knows ... to one who does not know...'. In their study they argued that it is time to 'de-couple' training and development in view of the differences in the two learning processes.

The amount of structure adopted

Professional development training is usually carried out in large groups in lecture or seminar format, which is then dominated by the view of the trainer (Clark *et al.*, 1984), rather than small, less formal structures. Many trainers use videos, presentations and structured discussions in their training programmes.

This is in complete contrast to personal development groups which can range from short three-day workshops to a twelve-month programme. Short programmes will cover communication, stress management, assertiveness; long programmes would probably include creating smaller self-development groups and supervision sessions for work related issues.

The structure of learning also varies where the highly structured format of professional skills learning is too rigid for dealing with the complexities and individual differences of personal development. Yet too loose a structure can also undermine the opportunity to learn, for example the group leader arriving in the group and saying 'The time is yours: what do you want to do?'.

The Difference between Therapy Groups and Personal Development Groups

Surprisingly, the boundary between personal development and counselling or therapy creates a very different comparison and on the face of it is less clearly defined. This is probably due to the many similarities between the two. Clarifying these similarities and differences should enable the personal development practitioner to work more potently.

Our focus here needs to be in comparing and contrasting the personal development group with group therapy. In any group work like this the group creates a background in which the individual can discover and understand themselves within a social reality. As a way of comparison we will first look at the similarities between these two types of learning groups shown in Table 7.2.

Looking closely at these similarities we see that it is the group process and the role of the group leader, rather than the content (i.e. the emerging issues) where therapy groups and personal development groups compare. This helps the group leader immensely as it clearly suggests that it is mainly (but as you will see later, not entirely) the content of the work that creates the difference and the boundary between these two

Table 7.2 Similarities between a therapy group and a personal development group

---

Facilitator must manage both process and content

Group leader to create a structure in which individuality and creativity can be fully expressed

The facilitator and the group form part of the learning process. They are a whole system

The group dynamics generate events which provide extensive learning material

Both groups will work with the here and now

Both groups are concerned in raising awareness of the whole person, then expanding individual work into the group learning

The issue of letting go of dependency on the group leader is a fundamental part of the group process

The group members are available for creative experimentation for the development of individual members

There is the potential for individual development at all levels (intellectual, behavioural, emotional, spiritual)

---

arenas as set out in Table 7.3. In this table we begin to identify the key differences in both structure and process for the group leader. Developing people in organisations is structurally determined by the organisation: the priority is to support the business. Therapy groups largely exist to support mental health and people in community, so are structurally determined by the community and the people who run them. Personal development programmes in organisations are intrinsically linked to business success, so the focus, to a large extent, will be determined by business needs – not individual needs. Individual needs are met within the confines of the programme. This is not so in a therapy group.

The Skilled Facilitator

Bringing together the being self and the doing self in organisational work to form something new, requires

Table 7.3 Therapy groups and personal development groups

Therapy group	Personal development group
Engage mainly with the being self	Engage with both the doing and the being self
Work extensively with archaic material for example from childhood	Only raise awareness of archaic material to create insight, understanding and generate behavioural change in current and future situations (referred to therapy)
Themes tend to emerge from the group process	Themes for learning frequently pre-determined, only occasionally are organisational groups set up as purely personal development groups
The frame in which the group leader works is based on their specialist skills, e.g. gestalt, transactional analysis, Rogerian or an integrated approach The theme is always therapy	The framework of the programme will be based on the theme (as defined by organisational needs) as well as influenced by the specialist skills of the group leader(s)
Run over a long (often indefinite) period of time	Frequently short, modular courses (i.e. stress management) unless defined as a personal development programme which may run for 12 months or more
Work with regressive states	Do not work with regressive states although identifying developmental deficiencies for reparatory work as an adult may be part of the personal development (e.g. developing potential for being creative)
Contracts are only with group memebrs so individual and group needs are the focus of the leader's attention	The group leader will need to accommodate both the individual needs of group members and organisational needs (re contract with the client)

- a good depth of self-understanding
- an understanding of organisations and organisation culture
- good management of the two boundaries addressed here
- a good range of skills for creative intervention
- flexibility and range

Working with Boundaries

In professional development there is an expectation from the trainee that the group leader is there to provide the information. The role of the leader is to teach skills and techniques in such a way that trainees know how to apply the learning themselves when they return to their workplace. Therefore it is quite appropriate for the leader to take on the role of expert (Clark *et al.*, 1984).

This can become a trap in personal development programmes. The inexperienced or attention-seeking group leader may inappropriately (there are occasions when this is appropriate) take on the role of 'expert' or 'guru' or become hooked into 'feeding' information to group participants who are more familiar with skills training and who have an expectation that the leader will provide, creating a dependency on the group leader.

> I (Clayton) fell into this trap in my early days of facilitating development groups. When feeling ill at ease it helped me (so I thought) if I could produce new knowledge for trainees to ingest, rather than staying with the discomforts of the group and working with the body of rich material available. It helped me temporarily but reduced the opportunity for personal development of the group.

When this happens you, as the group leader, are drawn into using theory and working at an intellectual level, rather than being creative with the group in a more holistic way and at a personal level. You leave yourself open to attack by the (now confused) group (seeing you as a 'professional' rather than as yourself). Group members lose an opportunity for personal development because of the dependency that you have created. The frame of work becomes distorted. The boundary between professional development and personal development confused.

The reverse may also happen, where a consultant familiar with the processes of personal development is asked to teach professional skills. If personal or group issues arise (relating to the being part of the self or group), which get in the way of learning, then these will need to be addressed. However, if too much time is given to the personal or group issue then time for professional skills becomes limited. The skill of the group leader is in dealing with the issue enough to re-establish the full potential for professional learning within a limited time frame. Good intervention skills can enable this to happen.

'Self-awareness and flexibility are the keys to good facilitation in either of these situations:' The key to good facilitation in either of these situations is self-awareness and flexibility: identifying and acknowledging when you and the group are slipping over the boundary, then using flexibility in your management of this.

Case Study

Sally was asked to run a series of finance courses for a local education institution. She has the competencies to work with both personal and professional development and was well able to run a programme on finance for the chosen group. However, on the first day she discovered that many of the trainees had been 'sent' on the programme rather than making that choice themselves. This evoked a lot of anger in the group. Sally thought that she could either continue with her designed programme and fulfil the needs of some of the group (and her contract with the organisation), or stop and address the issue fully so that it didn't get in the way of learning for everyone. She chose the latter but was clear with the group about boundaries (she stated that she would allocate a certain amount of time for the group to deal with this issue; her expectations of the group; and her intentions to resume the contracted programme). She was creative with her interventions and careful in managing the time spent addressing the problem.

She was working on the boundary between professional and personal development, her contract with the group and client; was for professional development. To overstep this contract with the group and the client could have undermined her credibility as group leader and reduced the potential for learning even more. The way around this was to negotiate with the group time to deal with the feelings evoked by 'being sent' before continuing with the contracted programme.

One of the criteria for maintaining good boundaries is for the group leader to be explicitly clear about the learning boundaries at the beginning of the training, as well as demonstrating maintenance of these boundaries throughout. Other than professional boundaries these might include time-keeping, personal responsibilities and confidentialities.

As a group leader, you need to have had considerable personal development yourself. For you can only enable others to develop, to the extent to which you have managed to develop yourself. That is your limit and your boundary. So if you find getting in touch with your feelings difficult and have not dealt with this, then it will be difficult to help others do the same.

Secondly, personal development groups will benefit greatly from your experiences, combined with a good sense of self-awareness; the wider your experiences, the greater the benefit to others. From this interventions will emerge, not simply from technical skills but also from a fullness of life, achieved through struggling, making errors, learning to be a human being (Zinker, 1977). This also enables the group leader to be clear about their own boundaries, especially their own limitations and vulnerability.

The extent to which you have dealt with your own issues will give you some indication of your boundaries with others. If you have just started work on your own personal development, then your work with others will be limited. It is a myth that those who have experienced tragedies, deprivation, abuse, redundancy and relationship problems are the best people to help others who have had similar experiences, unless they have learned how to deal with them effectively themselves.

So when we speak of working within boundaries in organisational work we are not just talking about clearly defined working boundaries agreed with the group, like time boundaries or structural boundaries, we are also talking about those discussed here and the boundaries of your own personal limitations. In the interest of the group it is worthwhile making explicit these boundaries and the risks involved when working with personal development. You then begin to build in a safety element and open up choices for group members, enabling some personal control over their own development. This also is good expectation management and develops a working alliance between you and the group at a very early stage.

Managing the Professional Development and Counselling Boundaries

Once in the personal development role you are like a skipper steering a boat, your seamanship skills allowing you to move with ease between being and doing, heart and head, love and will. Bringing the boat back on course when the undercurrent momentarily pulls away, guiding the individual and the group back into the personal development arena. Good seamanship skills involve recognising when the boat is going off course and knowing what to do (appropriate interventions) to correct that. Of significant importance here is in working with permeability rather than in a prison. Developing a range of skills with which you can cross all three arenas and still remain congruent with yourself. That entails working with your own 'personally developed self' where the professional and the personal part of you work together in unison. This also involves being seen in your wholeness, therefore not establishing a position as guru or expert, for that would lead you straight into the professional development arena, but allowing yourself to be human, with your skills and knowledge flowing through you. Working with a range of possibilities in a flexible way.

Experience indicates that generally different types of interventions are required to manage the two different boundaries. The following will give you examples of these.

When you are invited (seduced or coerced) into the professional development arena

Symptoms of the group – intellectualising, theory seeking, putting you

Professional and personal development

on a pedestal, talking 'about ...', demanding structure, presenting selves in role rather than as a human being, wanting tasks.

Intervention: Bring the person and the group into the here and now

> 'So as you talk about that, what is happening to you now? '
> 'I notice as you said you glanced over to Sally , is there anything you want to say to her ?'
> 'How do you think your theory applies to this group?'

Intervention: Normalising

> (Redundancy/demoted) 'It's normal to have feelings like this.'
> (Coping with change) 'Most people would experience difficulties going through as many changes as you have.'
> (Team splitting up) 'I imagine others in your team are feeling sad as well, have you asked them?'

Intervention: Work with the task vs. process polarity

Both task and process are important, learning how to move rapidly between them without staying too long with one or the other is an excellent skill for the personal development group leader. This also prevents you from being seduced into the professional development arena. Encouraging the group to look at their own process instead of you instigating it is even better.

Intervention: Interpretation

Interpretation of the group process or individual position can induce a new, more powerful perspective.

> 'People in this group seem to be concerned with ...'
> 'It sounds to me like you are angry with the way you were fired as well as distressed at not having a job.'

Intervention: Modelling

Modelling is a good process to use where professionals find it difficult to get in touch with themselves i.e. self-disclosure, spontaneity. It prevents them from only seeing you as a professional, is very permission giving and demonstrates 'how to' for those who have never tried or learned. Once they begin to practise this, reinforcement from you will aid development and also model to the group the reinforcement process.

> 'That was a lovely thing to have said to Alan.'

'Have you noticed that you are much more effective when you respond spontaneously rather than when you edit what you are going to say?'

'I feel angry when you speak to me like that.'

However, as group leader, you must be aware of the appropriateness of revealing yourself to the group through self disclosure. Too much will have the opposite effect, with you losing the respect of the group.

Intervention: Structural

Creative exercise using key discussion points can bring the group back into the here and now and enable people to get in touch with themselves.

For example, a group member has spent some time talking 'about' assertiveness, which eventually leads to her concerns about not being assertive herself. An exercise could involve her practising her assertiveness with members of the group and the group giving feedback, or where other group members also identify with this, for the whole group to move into pairs and practise being assertive with each other. A further possibility would be to work with micro skills development where the group and their leader give spontaneous feedback to the individual who is working.

Case Study

Anna brought an issue to her supervision group in which she was about to negotiate for work with a male client who she believed could easily undermine her position, leaving her floundering. Instead of spending too much time talking about the problem, the group set up a scenario where Anna initiated a male member of the group into the role of her client. She did this by standing behind him and saying 'you are (tall, powerful, sexist, will use your charm and position to manipulate me)'. She then set the scene and role played with her client what she imagined the conversation would be. The group and the supervisor stopped her every time she did or said something which would reduce her position of influence. The group would then look at how else she could have been different, and she would replay using new language, behaviour, or body posture. This process exposed a number of issues around the way Anna communicated situations where she needs to be influential; it touched on issues which she thought she had resolved. Anna maintained a confident and influential position throughout her meeting with her client and did not feel undermined by his manipulative manner.

Intervention: metaphor

One of the strengths of using metaphor is the many layers that exist and

Professional and personal development

can be worked with. Encouraging metaphor enables people to explore difficult issues in a safe way. We live in a world of metaphor, they operate at our fingertips, yet people often shy away when specifically requested to use metaphor. Using life and work experiences can help, especially where people are less able to visualise: for example, for someone who works with computers it may be useful for them to describe or draw their experience in terms of 'menus', 'thread structures' or commands. Use of available items in the room, i.e. pencils, paper, other objects or clothes, can all bring the issue into the here and now. Once the translation into metaphorical terms has been made, people can choose at which level to work with their issue – including skilled interventions by the facilitator to steer them away from unhelpful ground; with the individual still owning their metaphor. Such interventions will be based on your own observations, such as:

> 'Tell me more about ... (a specific image in the metaphor)'
> 'You skipped over ... when you described your image'
> 'How does this image compare with your experience in this group/your team?'

When you are seduced into the counselling arena

Symptoms; catharsis seeking, excessive release of feelings, working with issues only related to the personal self, constantly being pulled towards historical and childhood events.

Intervention: De-personalising

De-personalising can be achieved through theory interventions or turning the problem into a story, i.e. creating a metaphor of organisational change or symbolisation. This keeps the validity of what is being said and retains a connection with the group.

Intervention: Normalising

Normalising and generalising, especially involving the group, can be extremely useful, and, with sensitivity, can also provide support and empathy.

> 'It's normal to feel like this when working under such pressure, I imagine other members of the group experience similar feelings as well ? ...You could ask them'.'
> 'I feel really sad when I hear your story, I imagine there are many people out there in the same boat, yet somehow it seems more real when I hear you talk about it'.

Intervention: Relate the issue to the working environment, especially relationship issues

> 'So you have a problem speaking out in this group which you say is related to

your childhood. I imagine you have the same problem at work.'
' ...well, your boss isn't your father, so maybe you could experiment with ways of working with your boss more effectively.'

Understanding human relationships at work is key to personal development in organisations.

Intervention: Structural

Change the seating, configuration or membership of the group or organisation. Ask the manager to leave; two rivals to encounter each other directly, facing each other with eye-contact and expression of their feelings and doubts; the consultant physically standing in front of someone who is at that moment being scapegoated – these are all examples of structural interventions.

Intervention: Prescriptive

Where deep issues are revealed and you believe that therapy would help, you can say 'I believe this is an issue that could be dealt with in therapy' offering assistance to put them in touch with someone if required. This acknowledges their issue and offers support, without overstepping the boundary.

Maintaining good boundary management is an area for continued development and supervision, for people who work with personal development of others. Each situation, each group and each organisation is different. New challenges face us every day, as we expand our understanding of the relationship between people, systems and business. Our changing social systems – crossing cultural boundaries around the world – present new and challenging dynamics for facilitators to address themselves – their own prejudices, their abilities to engage with diversity, their willingness to confront new boundaries like religion, colour, age, gender, race. Our own learning and development about ourselves must take precedence before we can facilitate the personal devlopment of others.

Conclusion

Would that it were so simple – that knowing this would make the problems go away. It is daily, minute by minute work. Of course the boundary is fluid, moving, dynamic and yet it must be there. Working with and around it may just be the consultants life's work. The group or the organisation can take their share of responsibility by keeping it under discussion whenever obviously relevant and particularly when it appears not relevant.

References

BAC (1989). Invitation to Membership, Form No. 1. British Association for Counselling, Rugby.

Boydell, T. Leary, M. Megginson, D. and Kedler, M. (1991). *Developing the Developers.* London: Association for Management Education and Development.

Clark, N. and Phillips, K. with Barker, D. (1984). *Unfinished Business.* Aldershot: Gower.

Clarkson, P. (1991).'Counselling, psychotherapy, psychology and psychiatry', *Employee Counselling Today,* 3(3), 10-18.

Clarkson, P. (1994). 'The nature and range of psychotherapy', in P. Clarkson and M. Pokorny (eds) *The Handbook of Psychotherapy.* London: Routledge.

Harrison, R. (1983). 'Strategies for a new age'. *Human Resource Management* 22(3), 209–35.

Johnson, R. A. (1991). *Owning Your Shadow.* New York: Harper Collins.

Phillips, K. and Shaw, P. (1989). *A Consultancy Approach for Trainers.* Aldershot: Gower.

Zinker, J. (1977). *Creative Process in Gestsalt Therapy.* New York: Vintage.

Chapter 8
The pseudocompetent executive: Achilles at work

PETRŪSKA CLARKSON

The Problem

Many people in organisations secretly fear that they are incompetent in some way. It may be phrased as 'fear of being found out' or 'fear of being a fraud'. Surprisingly, such undermining tensions often affect those who have a reputation of excellence in their fields. This chapter explores the 'Achilles syndrome' – an increasingly common complaint of a crisis of confidence. Psychologically it is described as the condition when winners feel like losers.

Introduction

This Chapter examines rapidly changing current organisation culture and how it encourages and maintains large-scale pseudocompetency among the workforce, particularly among the senior people in the organisation. Pseudocompetency is defined as the experience of a big difference between people's own (low) assessment of themselves and others' (high) opinion of them in their particular field. Shame is discussed as a means of perpetuating individual and corporate pseudocompetence.

Changing Organisations

As a counsellor and psychotherapist, I have become increasingly aware of the large-scale disruptive impact that current world conditions have upon my clients, most of whom are well-functioning and intelligent professionals. As an organisational consultant, I am increasingly perturbed by the depression, fear, anger and bitter disillusionment of many people with the organisations for which they work, or from which they are being 'out-placed' or being made 'redundant'. This is based on extensive experience of working as an organisational consultant and trainer to large organisations and to their own trainers and consultants. The following conversation between client and counsellor is typical:

A: I'm scared at work. Scared of talking and having people take me seriously. I've got to perform, doing something I'm not sure I can do.
B: If people take you seriously you have to perform relentlessly at that level.
A: I can't keep it up because I'm not allowed not to know something.
B: But at some point or another you are bound to come across something you don't know!

Managers and developers need to enable themselves and empower others to survive these turbulent, unpredictable conditions and transform them into opportunities for survival, if not growth. The natural human need for security, control, certainty, and predictability is denied again and again as institutions go out of business and economic conditions fluctuate unpredictably. What used to be a reasonable expectation, for example a lifetime of employment, is now constantly under review. Even the last bastions of the public sector can no longer be sure of this.

I repeatedly hear people say, 'We just don't know what sort of job we will have in the future, or in a few months' time. There seems to be no leadership. We are given impossible tasks. Our targets are increased, resources lowered, employer expectations seem to be escalating, and we feel crazy because we're expected to do what cannot be achieved.' I am reminded of Pavlov's dogs who were rewarded for successfully differentiating between an ellipse and a circle; as the experimenters gradually shaped the ellipses into circles and the circles into ellipses, the dogs experienced the impossibility of the task and essentially went mad. This is how some people describe their working conditions now.

At the same time as such conditions of precariousness, uncertainty and stressful anxiety become the norm for a very large section of our working population (including the top managers) there is an escalation in complexity on all fronts which may leave us feeling even more deskilled. As one person said, 'Even if you don't change, change is being foisted on you'. Continuity is over, and the 'management of change' has become a contradiction in terms. Long-range unpredictability has become the norm and the only constant now is change itself. At a workshop for managers, one participant examined the personal cost of her professional pseudocompetency: 'I was making the hurdles higher and higher. Last year I did not jump them – I crashed spectacularly. Looking back, my greatest sense was relief; it would have given me a promotion I was not ready for.'

The Need to Make Meaning

The two most basic psychological needs of human beings are to work and to love. Work is one of the most important ways of gaining our sense of efficacy, competency or mastery in the world. Child development researchers confirm what common sense has always known – that people need to make some kind of useful contribution to the world in order to maintain their self-esteem. This need is apparently universal and unrelenting, although the definition of work is of course very wide – it may be housekeeping, caring for an elderly parent, voluntary service, creation of a multi-million-dollar business empire, doing a newspaper round or singing in a choir. When people lose this sense of making a valuable contribution, they often get depressed, and may even lose the will to live.

When people are deprived of the opportunity to work through their feelings about retirement, redundancy or loss of a job, the psychological damages are profound. Statistics show how many men die within two years of retirement – a shocking figure. It may relate to the fact that many of these men report that, although they may be happy to stop the pressures and strains of their work, they miss the company at work, the social side, the feeling of being significant to others, the challenges which they used to resent, but which gave them a sense of achievement and satisfaction. The psychological, economic and social ravages of redundancy in some parts of Western Europe have created a veritable industry in counselling services related to employment, re-employment and self-marketing. These all focus on – and sometimes exploit – the human horror of empty hours and a meaningless existence. Being accepted for just being yourself is essential, and should not be confused with being valued for your production or contribution.

The costs of loss of work are enormous. Losing a job can mean you lose status, money, company (both social and collegial), strokes, meaning and value in our society all at one go. A man who loses his job is in a time of great need for support and companionship, yet one such man told me that he could not face going to the pub to see his friends because they all knew he had lost his job. He could not even face their sympathy, he felt so bad. Yet these were in fact the people he could probably count on for support, advice and networking towards finding the next job.

What is Pseudocompetence

We are pseudocompetent when there is *a mismatch between our own self-confidence in a particular field and our competence in it as assessed by others*. This causes the discomfort or distress many people experience when the internal and external assessments are very dissimilar or contradictory. *Competence* means being able to tackle a task well, both subjectively (as assessed by self) and objectively (assessed by others). Competence means your inner confidence is well-matched with your performance. *Incompetence* is used here, not as an insult, but as a pointer that further development is needed in order to meet objective competency criteria. It means that you don't yet know how to perform well in the particular area. Acknowledging incompetence here means the beginning of learning is possible.

In the current professional climate there is enormous interest in professionalisation. Many structures are being created for judging competence as objectively as possible in various fields by boards, groups, and examination structures. Increasing professionalisation is evident in most fields of human endeavour. Accompanying this is a growing appreciation of and even legal insistence on re-accreditation in the professions, and annual competency reviews in organisations. So it is no longer the case that people can train or qualify and be considered competent for all their lives. There is even discussion about regular *re-testing* to establish competency to drive a car.

These initiatives may be partly in response to the recognition that conscious competency is a stage in an ongoing learning cycle which almost inevitably fades into unconscious incompetence unless skills are reviewed, attitudes re-assessed and knowledge updated.

Of course, along with this enhanced interest in professionalisation, externally assessed competency criteria and re-accreditation, there is now a growing disquiet among many professionals which they find hard, if not impossible, to admit. This may partly be a defence against the fear of pseudocompetence. It also simply places the fear elsewhere, such as, 'Will I be in or out of the socially agreed-to-be-competent group?' To be a top manager in many commercial competitive organisations means that you know how to manage in all ways at all times. You would never show that you feel inadequate, insecure and full of doubt about your capacity to do parts of your job.

As one top management trainer said to me, 'As I realise that I am acquiring a "good" reputation professionally, I feel an equal mixture of pleasure and fear. In paying attention to the whole of my person, including the feelings in my body, I began to realise the difference between pseudocompetency and created competency'. Many people have difficulty admitting this. Most people don't know that there is any alternative to pseudocompetency because many of our educational and training programmes train people in pseudocompetency. Many parents, trainers and teachers themselves are pseudocompetent, so it is a self-fulfilling cycle. A police officer told me how, in his view, pseudocompetency in his organisation had become institutionalised, for people were not staying in one job long enough to learn how to become fully competent at it before moving on within the organisation.

On encountering the notion of pseudocompetency, people are often tempted to apply it as a way of understanding other people, or as a diagnostic tool. This would not be correct since the idea concerns a subjective experience. Since it is really the *experience* of a mismatch between how confident a person feels and how they appear to perform any assessment, it is to be named by the person concerned in the privacy of their own heart. We should consider the major part played by the workplace in fostering pseudocompetency in the working context. Our society has inherited organisations characterised by shame and shaming systems. Indeed, shaming is probably the greatest single cause of pseudocompetency in the workplace. Shaming is often a covert strategy adopted by the organisation in the false belief that the fear of shame will make people perform more efficiency. Experience has shown that motivation based on fear may work in the short term; but in the long term this is more often than not highly dysfunctional. Shame is also used within some of the more competitive working environments as a way of exercising power and control. It would thus be counter to the spirit and intention of this idea to apply the term pseudocompetent to colleagues at work, since this may be helping to create the very condition of shame that fosters pseudocompetency in the first place.

Organisational trainers, managers and workers have told me that on training courses it is frequently considered shameful to admit that you don't know how to manage, how to motivate people, or how to resolve interpersonal conflicts. Of course it is very hard to train people to be better at something if they are not even prepared to admit that there is room for improvement! Business cultures easily collude, making it difficult, if not impossible, for people to go through the different and difficult phases of learning. 'When people see what I can do, I think inside "Oh no, not you as well!" I've learnt now to say no to people. Before, I was sending out very powerful invitations to people to say "You can do it". Now I have learned to function well under stress, even if I'm ill-prepared. That too is a cover-up.'

'Competence' in such organisations comes to mean the way in which you hide the fear of being in a situation in which your competency is being judged. Some people mistake competency itself for whether or not you can give an 'acceptably polished' performance. If you can 'fake it', then that makes you a good professional. Whether or not we actually know the job is sometimes considered less important than *creating the impression* that we know the job. A key concern at interviews of a company's hiring team is: Is this person acceptably professional in the commercial environment? Much discussion (in management consultancy as well as in other forms of sales) is devoted to the presenting persona of the management consultant or the salesperson.

> 'I put together some community programmes. They were basically OK but they had no depth. I never wrote it up because I couldn't – I didn't have the backing or the understanding of what I was doing. It looked good but if you'd put your hand through there would have been nothing behind it, and it's such a shame because what I did was good but... Internally I knew that I was cheating. I knew that I was getting away with things all the time, but I felt good because I felt like I was one of them and getting a lot of satisfaction and strokes.'

The reality of covering up your inadequacies and insecurities is being

The pseudocompetent executive

judged; in other words, how well you can create an impression, or a favourable façade. A consultant told me, 'Many organisations have bought into the Emperor's new clothes syndrome; and yet every person knows the others are bullshitting.' This is pseudocompetency and how it is maintained in organisational life. I have also encountered several high-powered executives who are very embarrassed by the fact that they do not have degrees. They then attempt to hide the fact, lie, or buy degrees to compensate for this imagined inadequacy.

The taboo is on discussing what you don't know, admitting the flaw. Doing so proves you are incompetent, so nobody does. Wanting to talk about it in order to get help, you feel trapped in the pretence and eaten up by the anxiety of being found out. 'On no account say that anything is an experiment – we are not trying out anything – we know what we are doing, and this must be adhered to'. 'We simply can't accept trial and error'. Delegates to top European business training schools have said: 'We have to keep what we don't know hidden even from ourselves.' Another executive said

> 'I used to say to myself, I know some things and not everything – then the working day becomes stimulating. When I act in that way, I think that I'm working in an environment where people are acting in the opposite way. It's threatening to me. When I don't know what I'm doing here I look indecisive, and it's not OK to be like that. It's difficult and damaging. I was made redundant recently.'

Pseudocompetency often has more hold in the executive and professional groups where there is a lot of space for cover-up. There may even be a closing of the ranks to protect pseudocompetent colleagues of the same professional body because everybody fears their own inadequacies may be exposed if a fine-tooth comb is to be taken to any one in the community. Most people feel that they have covered up or skipped over some area in developing and getting recognition for their expertise. Both the medical profession and politicians are frequently accused of just such professional collusion to protect incompetent colleagues; and sometimes it may be true. Of the organisational skills one learns, how many are true group skills and how many are for survival in a collusively pseudocompetent atmosphere?

> 'I remember the anger when I was five at seeing my school report say how mature and independent I was. This is also the damaging aspect of organisational culture. I was appointed to train trainers. I felt in need of some training myself, so I approached my manager but he immediately said "No, you don't need that, from what I've seen. You do it very well". His good opinion of me was destroying me.'

In business there is a need to go back and learn the *same* things, or the *basic* things again. How rarely this is presented and understood. What shame there would be in going back to re-take the early exams!

And how can we turn around and ask for what we are already supposed to possess, and to be using every day? It is hard enough for some workers even to ask for what would be sensible to learn, as some older workers have found in struggling to understand the new computer technology that their younger colleagues grew up with. As one executive put it, 'When I have applied for jobs and then got them on the basis that I am competent, I simply don't have the option of asking to go back to basics, to get some training. I've dug myself a hole. But what else could I have done to get that job?'

A colleague told me how she applied for a job in America.

> 'This vacancy was for a level 4 social worker, which is the highest, but I didn't understand the numbered levels because we didn't have that. I thought it was the lowest so I applied. They just couldn't believe the cheek – that I had actually sent my CV – without ever looking into the system. They called me to interview because they wanted to see the person that could do a thing like that. They asked what I had thought when I saw this advert and what were the skills I'd offer if they gave it to me. Anyway – I got the job – they gave me a job as a welfare worker until I got my degree, then I could become a social worker. They helped me through my course and had me assisting a social worker which was very good for me. This is a real example where I could talk my way through that interview and pull the wool over their eyes, and I did – in some way I really did.'

As a trainer I have often noticed that there are few applicants to introductory courses, and many applicants to the courses billed as 'advanced', even though the same ground may be covered. The tendency is to assume that we have grasped the basics – and we may not even be giving ourselves a chance to know what the basics are.

Long-range Planning May Not be Helpful

The situation is considerably worse even than the perpetuation in the present of organisational cultures which encourage self-deception, bluffing your way to get the credits and a whole ethos which suggests that we can know everything. A multinational corporation with a turnover of £130 billion had an unpredictable and inexplicable drop in sales of 25% in one week, from which it never recovered. People in business and organisations report an escalation of similar or worse situations, making it more and more impossible to do the kind of long-range planning that was considered highly desirable some years ago.

Current awareness that everything is changing very rapidly and unpredictably creates huge anxiety. Putting out a five-or ten-year plan is a defence against this anxiety, but it is also very harmful as it can restrict the learning process. Many management and strategic consultants have discovered that creating long-term plans does act more as a defence against self-doubt and uncertainty in this way. When reminded of their stated plans and actually retrieving the documents created at the time it was frequently found that people had done completely different things – often to their own surprise (Stacey, 1991).

People have found it much more useful to create and discuss different future scenarios. I believe BP did so, in considering the fact that crude oil might suddenly increase in price dramatically and unpredictably. When the situation in the Gulf occurred they were prepared. Most managers do not take five-year forecasts seriously any more, and this is a move away from rigidity towards flexibility and a recurrent admission that we should always be learning (and unlearning).

However, as many managers and organisational consultants have found, it is very risky to stand up and say 'I do not know what is going on and I am not preparing plans'. Of course your clients will get rid of you. You have to go through incredible smoothing-over actions to pretend that we know what is going on. We have to participate in this kind of pretence because the majority of people are looking through an old-fashioned Newtonian lens. Some of us are starting to see through the new lens; but we have to keep it quiet because others will get too frightened if conventional wisdom were fundamentally questioned. Moult (1990) had the rare courage to write in a management journal, 'We don't know what is happening and we don't know what we are doing'. This could be the beginning of developing true competence in learning.

Gossip in Organisations

This atmosphere of confusion can easily lead people to pretend they know things, which is one of the grounds for gossip. This can be particularly damaging within organisations. If we are frightened of not knowing what is going on, we take little snippets of information and construct a reality on the basis of these morsels. Gossips are frightened to approach anyone and ask 'What exactly is going on?' because the version they have heard may be based on one person's hypothesis or fear and have no relation to the facts at all. They may want to look powerful as holders of confidential knowledge, and being 'in the know' may also make them sought after and praised by colleagues. Or they may have had a bad experience of approaching someone once in this way, offering the version of the story that they have, and being severely criticised or laughed at for what they believed.

Changing the Organisational Rules

I was told about a manager in the retail industry who is chaotic and erratic – but people who have trained with him have a reputation for being much more resourceful and in demand than the rest in their other companies. There are many jokes about him 'still having a job', but the people who can stand the pace talk of an atmosphere of excitement, uncertainty and creativity – anything but a 'holding environment' – which is always or mostly a false promise in our uncertain world.

Until now, management has been all about control; now it is about change and paradox. Given the current state of our world, it is probably far more helpful in the long run for organisational consultants to facilitate people by teaching them how to work with chaos, disorder and the unpredictable than to strive for false security. The old style of management does not equip people for the real world, but instead builds a dependency on these grandiose promises of stability in a world which is essentially unstable and creative rather than rule-bound.

Identification of this problem, which affects some of the most talented people in organisations, led to the development of theory and technology of learning cycles, and consultancy about the development, assessment and problems of competency. These are more fully explained in *The Achilles Syndrome: The Secret Fear of Failure* (Clarkson, 1994).

References

Clarkson, P (1994). *The Achilles Syndrome: The Secret Fear of Failure*. Shaftesbury: Element.

Moult, G. (1990) 'Under new management', *MEAD*, **21**(3), 171–82 (special edition on postmodernism).

Stacey, R. D. (1991) *The Chaos Frontier*. Oxford: Butterworth/Heinemann. Also personal communication.

Further Reading

Casemore, R., Dyos, G., Eden, A., Kellner, K., McAuley, J. and Moss, S. (eds) (1994). *What Makes Consultancy Work: Understanding the Dynamics*. London: South Bank University.

Chapter 9
Stages of group development and the group imago

A comparative analysis of the stages of the group process

PETRŪSKA CLARKSON

The Problem

People learn many different models of group development without necessarily comparing and contrasting them for their mutual usefulness. Also, what is useful and destructive to do (for the manager, consultant, group process facilitator) is rarely clearly explained. This chapter compares Berne's concepts of group imago adjustment with the stages of group development as conceptualised by Tuckman(1965) and Lacoursiere (1980). It utilises Berneian diagrams of group dynamics in order to explain the nature of the processes involved at different stages in the maturation of a group. It also considers some of the most relevant tasks of group leaders at the different stages, whether the group leaders be trainers, organisational consultants or group psychotherapists.

Finally, it summarises the most relevant constructive and destructive group leader behaviours at different phases based on extensive surveys gleaned over more than two decades from hundreds of practitioners and trainees in the fields of group work, organisational consultancy and group psychotherapy. It is not intended to be definitive, but to encourage readers to cooperate in developing this area of theory and practice.

Introduction

Human beings are born into groups, live in groups and have their being through groups. As leaders of groups – as psychotherapist, trainer or manager – we are dealing with people who have already been shaped and affected by their previous group experiences. It can be very useful to understand this in relation to the process a group goes through as it forms and develops over time. The group psychotherapist in particular functions at this fulcrum of human existence where there is the greatest potential for destruction or the greatest potential for healing.

Most important changes in human history (for good or for ill) have come about through individuals combining their forces in groups, whether it be that of a lynch-mob or a band of missionaries. Since the human being's first exposure to the human group is in that of the family (or orphanage), the primal group is also matrix for the most long-lasting and profound injuries or capacities. It is by virtue of this fact that the group is probably the most potent matrix for individual and societal change.

> The need for social contact and the hunger for time-structure might be called the preventive motives for group formation. One purpose of forming, joining and adjusting to groups is to prevent biologic, psychological and also moral deterioration. Few people are able to 'recharge their own batteries', lift themselves up by their own psychological bootstraps, and keep their own morals trimmed without outside assistance. (Berne, 1975, p. 217)

Eric Berne's major contribution to group psychotherapy was the development of the system of transactional analysis as a means for individual change in the group, but he was also interested in the theory of group process and the phenomenon of the group as a whole. He stressed that each group had its own distinctive culture, including the group etiquette, technical culture and the group character. These whole group descriptive categories obviously correspond to Parent, Adult and Child aspects of the individual personality. This distinctive personality configuration of the group as a whole is more than the totality of individual attributes. Yet it forms an unique and distinctive entity which endures over time, goes through predictable stages of development or maturation, and can be more or less 'ailing' or healthy.

A group can be defined as a collection of individuals who are in interaction with each other for an apparently common purpose. The notion of apparently common purpose refers to the fact that, although there may be a commonly agreed social-level definition of the task of a group, there may be very many conflicting, confluent or complementary ulterior level agendas at the psychological level of the group (see Figure 9.1). The particular gestalt (whole) of all the separate members' psychological-level messages forms the collective psychological group entity. A public structure of any group may be identified and consensually agreed (Berne, 1975, p. 327). The collective private structure of the whole group is much more complex and developmentally labile. Badly managed critical periods in a group's life will affect its future functioning just as certainly as ineffective parenting will affect an individual's subsequent social and psychological development.

Transactional analysis is primarily, though not exclusively, a method of group psychotherapy. Yet there seems to be a dearth of transactional analysis literature concerning group dynamics (Altorfer, 1977; Berne, 1975; Kapur and Miller, 1987), group-as-a-whole awareness (Berne 1977; Gurowitz, 1975) and stages of group development (Misel, 1975; Peck, 1978).

Many readers who are familiar with the vast literature on the subject outside transactional analysis may use this chapter to remind them of what they know, while some new relationships are being delineated. For those who are not yet initiated into the intellectually exciting and emotionally adventurous world of group dynamics and group maturation, this chapter may act as a motivator to explore the field.

This chapter is intended to consider developmental stages in groups from a comparative point of view, specifically comparing Berne's stages of adjustment of the group imago (1975) with the stages of development

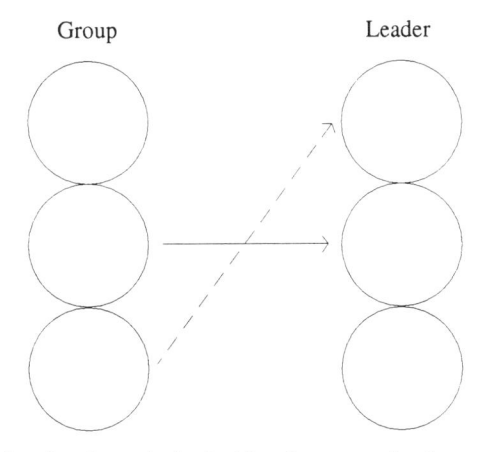

Figure 9.1 Social level and psychological level communication.

identified by Tuckman (1965). The fact that groups seem to go through predictable stages or cycles of development is very well established (Lacoursiere, 1980).

Although many authors have considered the stages, phases or cycles in the formation of a well-functioning group, most emphasise that these stages must emphatically not be seen as discrete or distinctly separate from phases which precede or succeed them. In a group such as a training group or a task group brought together for a specific purpose with a membership which remains constant from its inception to its termination, the separate phases are, however, often quite recognisable.

> Most groups and the individuals in them can be considered as going through a sequence of developmental stages during the group history or life cycle.

These stages – like most psychological and social processes – blend into each other to some extent so that where one divides one stage from the others, and how many divisions are made, depends partly on one's purposes, on how one views the data and so on. (Lacoursiére, 1980, p. 27)

Such predictable patterns in the evolution of a maturing group can be perceived by an initiated observer over the course of a three-year training or over the duration of an hour-and-a-half committee meeting. Knowledge of these phases is therefore relevant and potentially useful to any person who is either a member or a leader of any group of individuals for almost any conceivable purpose: from bringing up children to conducting an anti-nuclear demonstration to running a psychotherapy group. 'In therapy groups and T groups, the task is a personal and interpersonal one in that the group exists to help the individuals deal with themselves and others' (Tuckman, 1965, p. 385).

Novice facilitators often report some initial difficulty in managing the individual processes and individual contracts of clients alongside the necessity of managing the group process as a whole – that entity which is more than the sum of the parts of the individual members but upon whose health the wellbeing of all concerned depends.

In the closed psychotherapy group, the predictable stages can also be observed to the extent that the membership of the group remains reasonably stable and does not undergo major changes. However, it has often been noticed that, if several new individuals are introduced into a group, the group may need to regress to earlier and less developed levels of functioning and the group leader or group therapist may need to help the group re-cycle the different phases again. This is not dissimilar to the process involved in combining two families into one 'stepfamily' which almost invariably necessitates a re-working of identity, conflict management, rules and values, before they can come to a well-functioning state of effectiveness and interaction supportive to the individuals as well as to the family as a whole.

A theoretical understanding of these stages can help the group facilitator conceptualise occasionally baffling group dynamic phenomena, aid discriminating selection of techniques and interventions and find support in drawing on the experiences of pioneers in the field who faced similar moments of anxiety, despair, pleasure or pain.

Berne defines group imago as 'any mental picture, conscious, preconscious or unconscious, of what a group is or should be like' (Berne, 1975, p. 321). The group imago is an aspect of the private structure of the group and, therefore, may be differently perceived by different members at different phases of the group, although it may correspond very closely to the public structure. Imago adjustment is the process manifested in the observable stages in a group.

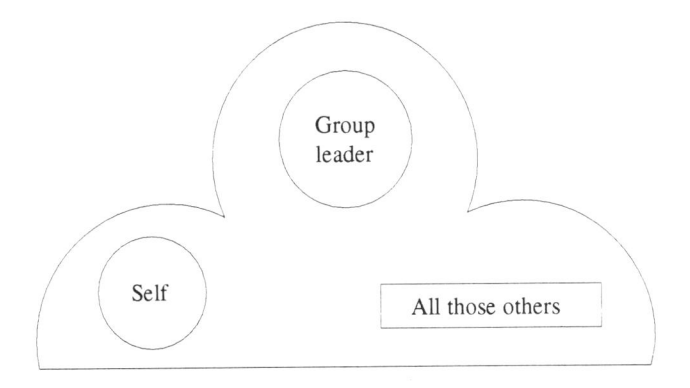

Figure 9.2 Provisional group imago.

Forming

The provisional group imago

> It should be clear now that each member first enters the group equipped with: (1) a *biologic* need for stimulation; (2) a *psychological* need for time-structuring; (3) a *social* need for intimacy; (4) a *nostalgic* need for patterning transactions; and (5) a *provisional* set of expectations based on past experience. His task is then to adjust these needs and expectations to the reality that confronts him (Berne, 1975, p. 221)

Before entering the group or before the group is activated, individuals form their own unique individual group imago of what it is likely to be like, based on their fantasies and previous experiences with groups, including their families of origin.

> As soon as his membership is impending, he begins to form a provisional group imago, an image of what the group is going to be like for him and what he may hope to get out of it. In most cases, this provisional group imago will not long remain unchanged under the impact of reality. (Berne 1975, p. 220)

The provisional group imago (see Figure 9.2) is suitable for structuring time through rituals. At this stage individuals are concerned with the nature and boundaries of the group task, they have fantasies about the ground rules and expectations of limits on behaviour based on past experiences of what is acceptable. A primary focus is preoccupation with and dependence on the leader in the beginning phases of a group. The individual's relationship to the group leader is likely to be of paramount importance. This is the most frequent vector for psychotherapeutic understanding and working through of transference, whether it be individual or the group-as-a-whole. This psychological emphasis is illustrated in the group imago by the placement of the leader in the upper slot.

It is interesting how this corresponds with projection onto the parent figure and the slots as Berne indicates them symbolically represent the projective spaces in which the individuals can project their grandfathers, siblings, teachers, and so forth.

In a small group, the central transference is on to the monitor but there is also the lateral transference of participants on to one another. This is due to the fact that in a small group participants rapidly get to know one another. There is also a third type, much harder to discern, analyse and interpret: the transference of participants (and the countertransference of the monitor) on to the small group as an object or entity. (Anzieu, 1984, p. 227)

In Tuckman's terminology the first stage, which apparently corresponds to the process of establishing the provisional groupings, is that which he calls *forming*.

> Groups initially concern themselves with orientation accomplished primarily through testing. Such testing serves to identify the boundaries of both interpersonal and task behaviors. Coincident with testing in the interpersonal realm is the establishment of dependency relationships with leaders, other group members, or preexisting standards. It may be said that orientation, testing, and dependence constitute the group process of forming. (Tuckman, 1965, p.396)

The process by which the provisional group imago is changed is influenced by member characteristics, but also by leadership tasks and behaviours.

Leadership tasks

In this stage the leader's most vital task is to deal with the external group process and define the major external and internal boundaries (Berne, 1975, p. 55). A physical and psychological external group boundary needs to be established which is secure and stable in order to ensure the survival of the group. Symbolically, the group therapist needs to create an alchemical container within which energy can be focused on the internal healing processes, safeguarded from external pressures.

There is an absolute necessity for clear contracts between the group members, the group leader, the group members with each other, and the group leader with his or her supervisor, co-workers, agency and/or landlord. The external boundary includes the physical space in which the group has its life. The unexpected arrival of the police at a seance is one of Berne's most vivid examples of how pressure on the external boundary of the group can lead to disintegration of the group. In another setting an imposed fire drill may precipitate different relationships from the usual coming to the fore in the group dynamics.

According to Gurowitz, the external boundary is largely a function of the internal boundary which he equates with the leader's potency. Therefore, a leadership task would be to create a strong and clear internal boundary which the group experiences as a barrier warding off external intrusions. 'In groups with a weak IB [internal boundary], the EB [external boundary] is seen as a fence confining members in an unsafe space' (Gurowitz, 1975, p. 184). One of the important factors in defining the major internal boundary is the psychological state of the leader or group psychotherapist. For example, a group leader experiencing a major bereavement would need to deal with the effects of this on the internal boundary of the group, both personally and collectively.

Other essential tasks of the leader at this point are to clarify 'who's in and who's out and who's in charge'. These considerations also define and safeguard the external boundary. Almost any group which meets on a regular basis will, with seemingly relentless energy, focus on absent members until all are properly accounted for. Having established that George is in Switzerland, May has taken her husband to hospital and Peter is late as usual, the group can settle down to its task, whether it is psychotherapy or a committee meeting.

It is equally vital for the group facilitator to define the boundary between the leadership region and the membership region, that is, which decisions and responsibilities are to be shared and which are the responsibility of the leader alone.

It is important for group workers and group members to decontaminate confusions between leadership and power. Often people call a group undemocratic on the false understanding that democracies have no leaders. The major difference between a democracy and an autocracy is that leaders in a democracy can be ousted by elective process whereas in autocratic situations this can only be done through violence and force. Leaders in organisations, such as managers, can often be removed through due process of disciplinary procedures. In most organisational or training settings, however, people can choose whether or not they participate.

Leadership needs to be balanced in such a way as to lead eventually to the empowerment of members. In a similar way to child development, leaders cannot responsibly avoid being leaders if that is what they are being paid for and if that is the psychological need of the group at its initial phases, just as a parent cannot abdicate all structuring and decision-making to an infant without endangering it. The task of the responsible leader involves, therefore, establishing rules, safety and boundaries. It may be necessary to establish dependency before resolving it. The group leader, like a parent, has to have the courage to allow him or herself to be loved, knowing all the time that the ultimate purpose is to lose this love.

Groups are often very anxious at the beginning of sessions or courses, so much so that experienced group leaders have learned that statements made in the first session will often not have been 'heard' by group members at this stage and may need to be repeated later when people are feeling less anxious and more relaxed. Excessive anxiety in the leader can be very disruptive and needs to be managed both in terms of his or her archaic personal issues in psychotherapy and in terms of concordant countertransference with the group process. The group conductor often embodies the cohesive forces of the group and may have sufficient or excessive investment (through fear of loss of reputation or income) in the continued survival of the group.

The group leader's task is to find an optimal level of anxiety for the group. That is, a level of arousal or investment which is conducive to maximum risk-taking and learning and yet not so extreme as to lead to incapacitation, re-traumatisation or the reinforcement of a destructive system. (A group may have a collective dysfunctional system in a similar way to an individual.)

What may appear to be a lack of structure may in fact be the imposition of quite a violent covert structure. Some of the casualties of the encounter group and T-group experiences of the 1960s were no doubt results of the tyranny of structurelessness. Indeed, Berne (1975) defines *structure hunger* as one of the basic hungers of the human being (pp. 215, 327) and *leadership hunger* as rooted in a leaders' responsibility to provide structure for the group within which its individuality and creativity can flourish (p. 216). In this way, as in many others, the role of group leader has similarities with that of a parent.

One of the most significant boundaries which affects the safety and trust of human beings is that of time. Carelessness around time is frequently reported as one of the more destructive group leader behaviours. Many psychotherapists who pay attention to the psychological level communication of their clients (Langs, 1978; Casement, 1985) corroborate the severe repercussions of confusing time structures.

In terms of complementary countertransference, group leaders may need to monitor their tendencies towards over-nurturing or over-control in the beginning stages of a group session or in the initial stages of forming a psychotherapy group.

Another important leadership task is clearly and visibly to assume responsible leadership. Some of the most destructive groups in people's experience are associated with situations where there was a confusion of roles and a reluctance or inability to be explicit about responsible leadership functions, appropriate delegation, decision-making, sanctions, and so forth.

Based on survey results over several years with hundreds of practitioners in organisational, psychotherapeutic or social work groups, the

Stages of group development and the group imago

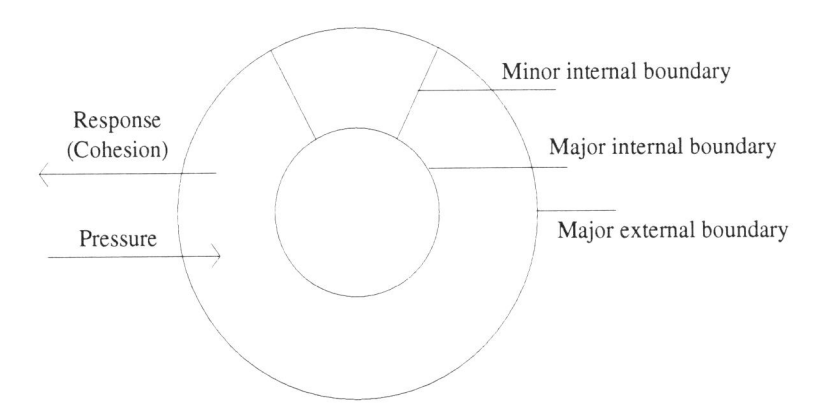

Figure 9.3 The external group process: Group cohesion vs. external disruptive forces.

behaviours and characteristics listed in Table 9.1 have been most frequently identified as more destructive or more constructive in the experiences of our respondents. Any or all of these behaviours may be relevant at all stages of group development. Also, most constructive behaviours could be destructive when used badly, mistimed or inappropriately in relation to different groups.

Equally many behaviours which are here listed as destructive may at times or in certain circumstances be useful, provocative or creative. Our results are summarised here more to act as a spur to thinking, a supervisory aid and a tool for self-exploration.

Table 9.1. Forming: destructive and constructive behaviours

Destructive behaviours	Constructive behaviours
Excessive anxiety in leader	Clear contracts – this is what the group is about
The tyranny of structurelessness	Clear time structure
Hidden sadism	Building optimal anxiety
Confusion about roles	Clear assumption of responsible leadership
Appears too aggressive or too seductive	Clarity of boundaries and clarity of group task
Too task-oriented	Facilitation of group members getting to know one another
Too many rules – too authoritarian	Early provision of practical/survival information, for example, toilets, breaks, food limits.
Focus on one person's pathology /acting-out behaviour at the expense of other members	Preparation of the room in a manner which demonstrates that group members are expected and welcome

Storming

The adapted group imago

The adapted group imago is 'superficially modified in accordance with the members' estimate of the confronting reality' (Berne, 1975, p. 321). It is particularly suitable for structuring time by means of pastimes. It is primarily characterised by agitation across the leadership boundary or the major internal group process (Berne, 1975, p. 55). The major internal group process results from conflicts between individual proclivities and the group cohesion as represented by the leadership and takes place at the major internal boundary, that is between members and the leader (see Figure 9.4).

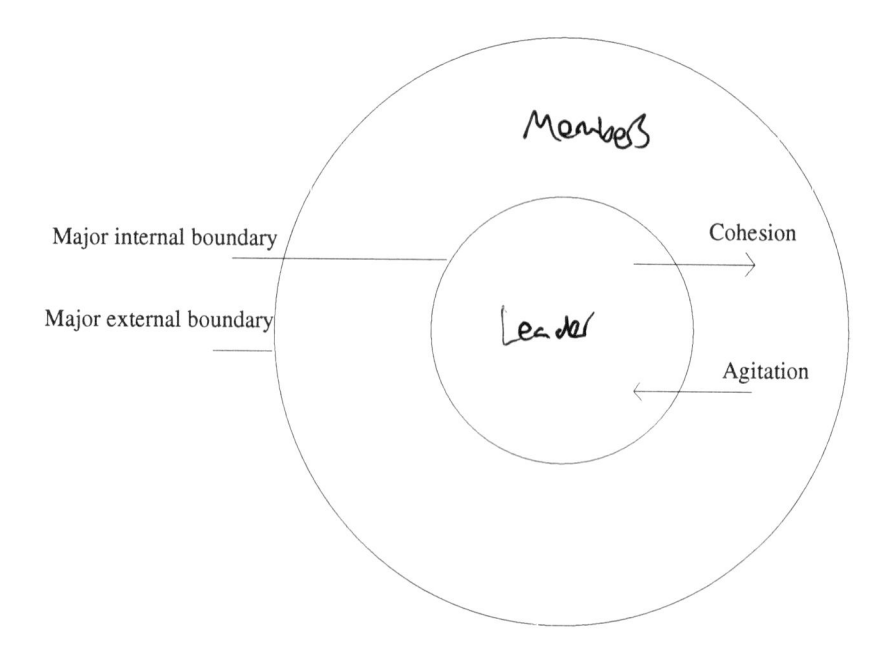

Figure 9.4 The major internal group process. Individual proclivity vs. group cohesion (characterised by agitation across the leadership boundary).

In Tuckman's terminology this second stage apparently corresponds to what he calls *storming*:

> The second point in the sequence is characterised by conflict and polarisation around interpersonal issues, with concomitant emotional responding in the task sphere. These behaviors serve as resistance to group influence and task requirements and may be labelled as storming. (Tuckman, 1965, p. 396)

This is probably one of the most important phases where conflict with, or rebellion against, the leader is a frequent occurrence. The stage is often referred to as 'the emotional response to task demands'. Storming is not always obvious in overt or covert criticism but may sometimes be manifested in depression, passivity and lack of energy in the group members.

The second phase in the development of the group imago is characterised by superficial modifications of the group imago in accordance with the members' estimate of the confronting reality.

Archetypically the effective leader in this stage is represented by the 'firm and fair' teachers that some people have experienced in their educational history. Experienced teachers often report that their relationship with the class can be made or marred in the first lesson. Group leaders can avoid overt storming by exploiting their own fears and vulnerabilities. An education tutor told the group that 'I hear you don't like me'; rescuers in her group told her what a nice woman she was but gossiped that they didn't really mean it.

The storming is frequently apparently about the nature of the task but psychologically is about the ability of the group leader to be effective. The storming phase is a necessary prerequisite to effective functioning later in the group life and probably as necessary as effective resolution of the 'terrible twos' rebellion in the young child. Storming is not to be seen as a distraction from the central task but a necessary stage in establishing the most efficient ways of conducting that task. This is a time when a group-leader's equanimity really gets tested.

Leadership tasks

The leadership task here (see Table 9.2) is to survive with the leadership boundaries and the group task intact at the same time as allowing individual members of the group maximum opportunity to test. The leader needs to survive verbal attacks from the group without punishing or collapsing, becoming neither punitive nor apologetic (e.g. 'I'm only trying to please you ...'). The feedback on leadership factors is less reliable at this stage because of contaminated projective colouring. Later in the development of a group feedback can be enormously valuable, but at this stage it is helpful for group leaders to give themselves the benefit of the doubt, while seeking both support and confrontation in supervision. It is important not to seek inappropriate support from the group or group members, and perhaps thus reinforce second-order structural symbiotic patterns.

Conflict and polarisation between members occur in response to adjusting their own needs to the task which does not fit the imago. Fight or flight might be predictable responses to anxiety and threat. In a consulting or training group this conflict or withdrawal may appear as resistance to change.

In groups where the leader is perceived as too frightening or too fragile to test or question, premature conflicts and polarisation may erupt

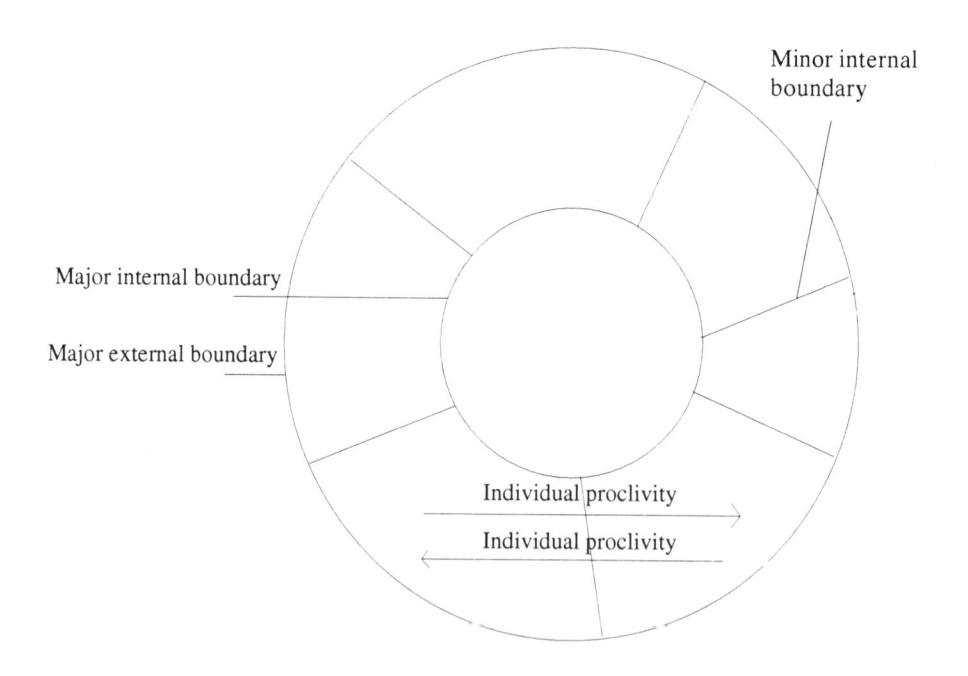

Figure 9.5 Minor internal group process. Individual proclivity vs. Individual proclivity.

Table 9.2. Storming: destructive and constructive behaviours

Destructive behaviours	Constructive behaviours
Leader who deflects or denies inter-group aggression and 'syrups over' conflicts	Taking people's feedback seriously without collapsing under the criticism
Leader interprets anger and rebellion as sign of individual pathology or of group sharing in a way which in validates or patronises members	Not giving in to blackmail, threats Validates people's right to their feelings, thoughts, opinions and concerns without giving up rights
Group leader looking too fragile, sick, appearing hurt	Mutual respect Ability to negotiate issues – to be flexible about negotiation for group to form its own particular culture
Taking any of four drama roles (Victim, Rescuer, Persecutor or Bystander) Ignoring the conflict – pretends it does not exist	Discriminates between compromises/ negotiations which would facilitate or handicap group task
Supporting polarisation or scapegoating No sanctions or unjust sanctions Abandons group	

between group members. Especially vociferous and apparently irreconcilable differences between group members in the initial phases of a group often mask unsatisfactory management of the storming phase by the group leader. Although it is not unheard-of, it is more usual for groups at the beginning stages to be involved with ritual.

> Similarly, in a psychotherapy group, an adaptable member will not begin to play his games until he thinks he knows how he stands with the leader. If he is arbitrary and not adaptable...he may act prematurely and pay the penalty (Berne, 1975, pp. 224–5).

The individual members of the group, unless seriously disturbed, will tend not to actively engage in second- or third-degree interpersonal games before having established the group leader's boundaries vis-à-vis themselves. For example, in a group of adolescents they may test the group leader by means of coming late, verbal abuse or indulging in antisocial behaviour such as glue sniffing.

In my experience, how the group leaders or unit managers deal with these early testing situations will, to a large extent, determine the subsequent response from the group members in terms of how they use the consultation or the activity group. Theoretically, every transaction that takes place in such a group is influenced by the transference – i.e. by the major process – but it is still possible in practice to separate the proceedings into those of the major internal process and those of the minor internal process; or, put in group dynamic terms, those in which individual proclivities are engaged with the group cohesion, and those in which two or more individual proclivities are engaged with each other. (Berne, 1975, p. 240).

Norming

The operative group imago

Operative group imago is 'further modified in accordance with the member's perception of how he fits into the leader's imago' (Berne, 1975, p. 321). Time is structured by means of undermining psychogical games.

In Tuckman's terminology this apparently corresponds to what he calls the stage of *norming*. Resistance is overcome in the third stage in which

> in group feeling and cohesiveness develop, new standards evolve, and new roles are adopted. In the task realm, intimate, personal opinions are expressed. Thus, we have the stage of norming. (Tuckman, 1965, p. 396)

This stage of the progression of the group imago is characterised by the development of group cohesion. This is where the games get played out and games and racket tolerance levels are established. Leadership hassles with the leader have successfully been worked through and interpersonal conflict either based on script replays of archaic patterns or here-and-now social skills learning can be constructively dealt with. There is a sharing of feelings and mutual support. A group in this stage has a clear sense of 'this is the way we do things around here'. Shared norms and values have been developed. The operative principle states that 'an adaptable member will not begin to play his games until he thinks he knows how he stands with the leader' (Berne, 1975, p. 225).

Table 9.3. Norming: destructive and constructive behaviours

Destructive behaviours	Constructive behaviours
Valuing rigidity	Members get recognised for making explicit queries around norming
No time given to norming	
Leader tries to set rules instead of norms and deny 'there is only one way to do it'	As a group leader, challenge norms to maintain flexibility
	Facilitate group developing own norms – norms are group's personality
Rigidity concerning rules such as 'there are no exceptions', no allowance for individual differences and individual needs	Flexibility around norms – and norm formation or culture-building not as pure introjection of unconsidered rules
Capriciously malevolent destructive members are allowed to stay and destroy group cohesion, task or procedure and process	Focuses on process of valuing
	Explicit statements of leader's values, e.g. race, sexual orientation
	Respect for each particular group's uniqueness

Leadership tasks

The leadership task at this stage (see Table 9.3) is the facilitation of interpersonal skills and modelling behaviours that will support constructive group norms. Effective leaders teach, for example, emotional literacy (Steiner, 1984) and provide information and resources. These can be particularly useful at this phase because group members are becoming more willing to use it constructively in a game-free way. The group imago is further modified in accordance with the members' perception of how they fit into the leader's imago. Leadership provides encouragement, modelling (providing value-congruent psychological-level messages) and process maintenance. Effective leadership can be said to be concerned with facilitating the healthiest forces within the individual or the group towards individuation and self-actualisation. In this sense the group leader has to be both potent in terms of having a clear set of explicit values and yet facilitate the group to develop its own norms as a manifestation of the group's personality.

The leader can set rules or contracts for which there may be sanctions, but norms can be influenced as the most potent factors in establishing a healthy group culture. There is some research which indicates that group norms are influenced not so much by what individual leaders say as by what they do. Often it is the throw-away comments or the peripheral management of boundary issues from which individual members draw conclusions about acceptable norms. In this way a group leader can challenge premature or oppressive norming to maintain flexibility and encourage members in informed and compassionate valuing processes, rather than norms based on rigidity, certainty and loudness.

Performing

The secondarily adjusted group imago

The secondarily adjusted group imago is 'the final phase, in which the member relinquishes some of his own proclivities in favor of the group cohesion.... The minor group process results from conflicts between individual proclivities and takes place at the minor internal boundaries' (Berne, 1975, p. 321) (see Figure 9.5).

In Tuckman's terminology this apparently corresponds to what he calls the performing stage.

> Finally, the group attains the fourth, and Tuckman's final, stage in which interpersonal structure becomes the tool of task activities. Roles become flexible and functional, and group energy is channelled into the task. Structural issues have been resolved, and structure can now become supportive of task performance. This stage can be labeled as performing. (Tuckman, 1965, p. 396)

Here the group functions effectively on their task, for example, training, with minimal interference from distracting group process and the group can now deal adequately with what arises with a reality orientation. In the counselling group, members achieve insight and behaviour change, and the task group engages in effective problem-solving.

This is the final phase in which the member relinquishes some of his own proclivities in favour of the group cohesion. Intimacy is possible between group members, and between the group members and the group leader at this phase.

The performing stage of a group has been satisfactorily achieved if the leader ends up surrounded by leaders and the psychotherapist by individuals who take responsibility for their own psychotherapy.

Leadership tasks

The leader's task (see Table 9.4) is to enjoy this phase and congratulate

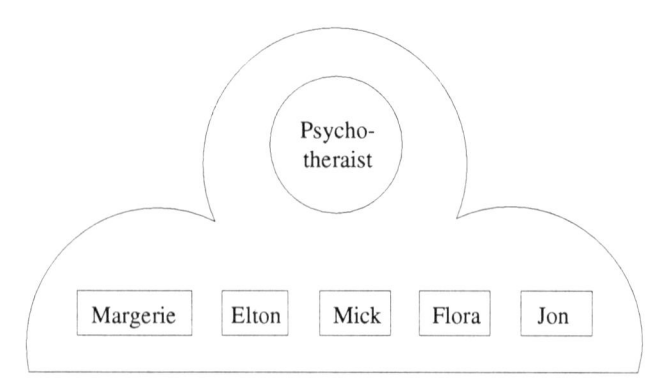

Figure 9.6 The differentiated group imago

Table 9.4. Performing: destructive and constructive behaviours

Destructive behaviours	Constructive behaviours
Criticises destructively, says 'I know better'	Sits back, relaxes, lets people get on with it, lets go
Puts people down	Allows people to be leading
Hogs credit	Becomes participant – joins group
Deprives group of autonomy	Leadership slot vacated to appropriate person, though ready to step in if necessary
Too keen on schedule	Offers praise, positive strokes
Persists in emphasising that he's in leader slot	Minimum control, maintains some safety boundaries – though group will usually do for self (time, refreshing, and so forth)
Tells people what they're doing isn't good enough	Says things like, 'Let's experiment with this'
Blemishing	Invites comment and evaluation, allows group to make choices
Holding too tight a rein	Within a wide range of open boundaries says what's permitted and what's not
Offers more punishment than reward	Relaxes, enjoys group
Stresses task and ignores maintenance	Permission to have fun and work
Is cool, impersonal and distant	Encourages and validates: autonomy, immediacy, authenticity, spontaneity, feelings, skills and knowledge
Refuses to listen to group members	Strokes for 'being' as important as strokes for 'doing'
Invalidates feelings	
Invokes drivers	
Invokes injunctions	

him or herself on satisfactorily having navigated the previous phases. Here you can really feel that you are doing the task well. Group members have ways of using their interpersonal processes to each other's benefit and although everybody may not be happy all the time, everybody is learning all the time.

After the difficult and delicate previous phases, the group leader or group psychotherapist can really enjoy this period. If a group psychotherapist has established this level of functioning in an ongoing group it usually will, to a large extent, maintain the established culture even through temporary separations, such as summer holidays, or minor fluctuations in group membership. To some extent, though, recycling or reworking of previous phases may recur, perhaps in a less obvious way, but the working through periods may tend to be shorter and the depth of discomfort/distress less intense.

It is important that the group leader let go of many leadership behaviours, allowing every member of the group to make leadership acts even as the group leader retains the responsibility. In successful and effective groups the leadership slot may be vacated and filled by one or more of the effective leaders in the group. Ideally, autonomous individuals will all be willing and able to make leadership acts on their own behalf and on the behalf of others for effective psychotherapy to take place.

Leadership tasks involve offering praise, positive strokes and minimising control while maintaining some safety – though the group will usually do this for itself – and offering structures and resources, saying things like 'Let's try this'. He or she invites comment and evaluation without holding too tight a rein and allows the group to make choices and decisions within a wide range of open boundaries regarding what is permitted and what is not. He or she relaxes, enjoys the group permission to have fun and work, and encourages and validates: autonomy, immediacy, authenticity, spontaneity, feelings, skills and knowledge. Finally, he or she joins the group as a whole person willing to be role-fluent.

Mourning

The clarified group imago

Although Berne only identified four phases as such, he defines 'The real aim of most dynamic psychotherapy groups is to clarify the group imagoes of the individual members' (Berne, 1975, p.241). Insofar as the group imago is a facsimile of an infantile group imago or a reproduction of a childhood group imago, its clarification and differentiation is part of the task of facilitating individuals and groups to live more of their individual lives in groups which are geared to their current here-and-now needs and to reduce or eliminate borrowed or anachronistic interferences with intimates, whether in the group or in life. If a group experience has been successful for a member it will usually result in a higher level of functioning and integration.

Some groups have as their major activity concerns with 'internal conflicts and concerts between forces, that is, in the internal group process, it may be called simply a process group' (Berne, 1975, p. 59). If this is the activity which operates across all stages of group development, withdrawal as a time structure becomes relevant and necessary at the termination of the group or the individual member's life in the group. 'Incidentally, a phantom is also left whenever a well-differentiated member leaves a group and persists until the mourning process is completed if it ever is' (Berne, 1975, p.225). Withdrawal is the divestment of emotional energy or cathectic charge from group cohesion.

The last phase is that of mourning (Lacoursiere, 1980) or adjourning (Tuckman and Jensen, 1977). The collective group focus is on termination. Psychologically, the group has to say goodbye and negotiate all the relevant grief processes.

Leadership tasks

Probably the most important leadership task (see Table 9.5) is to 'keep the group at it' and not allow individual members or the group 'to run away from' dealing with these issues at intrapsychic, interpersonal and group levels. It is expected that people may wish to avoid some of the pain of this period by making the group 'bad', blemishing the group leader, premature disengagement (physically by, for example, going sick or psychologically by, for example, 'It wasn't really important').

According to Worden (1983) the four major tasks of mourning are

- to accept the reality of the loss
- to experience the pain of grief
- to adjust to a changed environment
- to withdraw emotional energy and re-invest it in another relationship.

As the group terminates the leader's task is to facilitate the working through of such similar processes as they are manifested in the collective consciousness and avoidances of the group dynamic.

Kubler-Ross (1969) identified a five-stage sequence in loss:

- denial
- anger
- bargaining
- depression
- acceptance.

Such analogous phases of the grief process can be observed in some aspects or elements of the collective preoccupation towards the termination phases of groups, for example, idealisation prevents dealing with the sad feelings of separation by creating romantic ideas of reunions such as often happens on holidays with people to whom, if they did turn up on the doorstep back home, one would find that one had very little to say. Feelings that need to be dealt with at this stage include

- anger
- guilt
- sadness
- appreciation

The leader can give information about the process of grieving but also needs to facilitate the group to emotionally grapple with its implications.

The leader has personally to participate with mature emotions as well as intellectually in the process in order for the resolution to be effective in the same way as a parent needs to experience 'letting a child go' with the ambivalent feelings of sadness in the loss of a particular kind of closeness as well as pleasure in their independence. It is not infrequent for survival issues to emerge again at this stage.

Prediction can be useful. Every time people say goodbye, or separate from meaningful connections with others, they have an opportunity to re-live archaic separations in more healthy or creative ways, thus helping them to heal some wounds of the past, even if the short-term benefits are not immediately apparent. People have to say goodbye before they can say hello. Termination is often both deeper and more efficient if the group has been successfully managed.

This is where people have to let go of the group imago; hopefully it will have changed (see Figure 9.6) so that their next provisional group imago is based to a greater degree on trust in their own capacities and in other people's rational good will.

The successful group leader will allow individuals to handle grief in their own way without being persecuting about mourning. It is important not to go along with group denial (collusion) but to work out problems with endings vicariously through the group. It is also vital not to behave defensively at the blemishing stage but to listen and receive feedback; to support realistic plans for the future connected with endings;

and to predict varied reactions and allow ambivalence to be expressed. Ample time must be allowed for processing at this stage, just as individuals who are demanding treatment need sufficient time. Group leaders must let members know well in advance of a definite finishing time, and it is their task to provide or facilitate leaving structures and rituals which are congruent with the group norms.

Table 9.5. Mourning: destructive and constructive behaviours

Destructive behaviours	Constructive behaviours
Being persecuting about mourning	Allowing individual to handle grief in own way
Going along with group denial (collusion)	Predicting varied reaction
Working out own problems with endings	Letting people know well in advance
Behave defensively at blemishing stage	Very explicit and honest about what he or she is doing
Packing in the information	Realistic plans for future connected with ending
No time for process	Allowing ambivalence to be expressed
Sickly sentimental prescribed mourning, e.g., all hug or all say something nice	Finishing at a definite time
Overly extends the mourning period	Knowledge of what leaving ritual is going to be
Too abrupt an ending, not allowing afterglow of satisfaction	Allows and encourages reminiscing
Over-indulgent or allowing of idealisation or 'splitting'	Graciously accepts appropriate recognition and appreciation from the group
	Focus on individuation, integration and generalisation
	Facilitates group to use his ending as a learning experience for future endings

Table 9.6 Summary diagram of stages of group development

Tuckman	Berne	Time structuring	Lacoursiere
Forming	Provisional group imago	Rituals	Orientation
Storming	Adapted group imago	Pastimes	Dissatisfaction
Norming	Operative group imago	Games	Resolution
Performing	Secondarily adjusted group imago	Intimacy	Production
(Mourning)	Clarified group imago	Withdrawal	Termination

Conclusion

When managers, group leaders or consultants are working within a developmental model, they have found it very helpful indeed. As with all solutions to particular problems, it contains within itself another problem: for example, the assumption of causal, linear, progressive, and left-hemispheric game-rules. Models which draw from quantum physics as well as chaos and complexity theory do not rely on these parameters and open up possibilities of working very differently with groups under different situations (see Chapter 10 and 12).

This chapter drew on similarities between Berne's concept of group imago adjustment with the stages of group development as conceptualised by Tuckman (1965) and Lacoursiere (1980). It highlighted some of the most relevant tasks of group leaders at different stages of the maturation of the whole group. It collated survey feedback from practitioners and trainees identifying more or less useful group leader behaviours at the different stages. Throughout the focus has been on considering how group-as-a-whole developmental phenomena can be understood and utilised as an adjunct to individual psychotherapy in the group, not a substitute for it.

References

Altorfer, O. (1977). 'Group dynamics: Dealing with agitation in industry groups', *Transactional Analysis Journal*, 7(2), 168–9.
Anzieu, D. (1984). *The Group and the Unconscious*. London: Routledge and Kegan Paul.
Berne, E. (1977). *Principles of Group Treatment*. New York: Grove Press (first published 1966).
Berne, E. (1975). *The Structure and Dynamics of Organizations and Groups*. New York: Grove Press.
Casement, P. (1985). *On Listening to the Patient*. London: Tavistock.
Gurowitz, E. M.(1975). 'Group boundaries and leadership potency'. *Transactional Analysis Journal*, 5(2), 183–5.
Kapur, R. and Miller, K. (1987). 'A comparison between therapeutic factors in TA and psychodynamic therapy groups', *Transactional Analysis Journal*, 17(1), 294–300.
Kubler-Ross, E. (1969). *On Death and Dying*. New York: Macmillan.
Lacoursiere, R. (1980). *Life Cycle of Groups*. New York: Human Sciences Press.
Langs, R. (1978). *The Listening Process*. New York: Jason Aronson.
Misel, L. T. (1975). 'Stages of group treatment', *Transactional Analysis Journal*, 5(4), 385–91.
Peck, H. B. (1978). 'Integrating transactional analysis and group process approaches in treatment'. *Transactional Analysis Journal*, 8(4), 328–31.
Steiner, C. (1984). 'Emotional literacy', *Transactional Analysis Journal*, 14(3), 162–73.
Tuckman, B. W. (1965). 'Developmental sequence in small groups', *Psychological*

Bulletin, **63**(6), 384–99.
Tuckman, B. W. and Jensen, K. (1977). 'Stages of small group development', *Journal of Group and Organizational Studies,* **2**, 419–27.
Worden, J. W. (1983). *Grief Counselling and Grief Therapy.* London: Tavistock Publications.

Chapter 10
A small kitbag for the future

Survival skills for the next century

PETRŪSKA CLARKSON

The Problem

Most people report that 'it's rough out there' and getting rougher. Some people, some organisations are nonetheless thriving. This is what I, at this time, think helps. It's called *future fitness*. Darwin's idea is that it is the fittest who shall survive. However, he did not mean strongest – which is the usual misapprehension and a false meaning. He meant those organisms which are most adaptable to changing conditions.

Introduction

I am writing these brief notes in a postmodernist mood. It is not my intention to provide a new truth or even a new version of the old truths. This is a collage, juxtaposing the past and the present, the thoroughly digested with the half understood, intuition with knowledge, and experience with received wisdom. There is no intention to lead, or to prescribe; only to stimulate and ignite, to perhaps prompt towards recognition.

Current Conditions

As a counsellor and psychotherapist, I have become increasingly aware of the large-scale disruptive impact current world conditions have upon my clients, most of whom are well-functioning and intelligent professionals. As an organisational consultant, I am increasingly perturbed by the depression, fear, anger and bitter disillusionment of many people with the organisations for which they work, or from which they are being 'out-placed' or being made 'redundant' or undergoing yet another restructuring.

The natural human need for security, control, certainty, and predictability is abrogated again and again, as institutions go out of business, and economic conditions fluctuate unpredictably. What used to be a reasonable expectation, for example a lifetime of employment, is now constantly under review. No one can be sure of it, even in the last bastions of the public sector. I repeatedly hear people say,

> 'We just don't know what sort of job we will have in the future, or in a few months' time. There seems to be no leadership. We are given impossible tasks. Our targets are increased, resources lowered, employer expectations seem to be escalating, and we feel crazy because we're expected to do what cannot be achieved.'

I am reminded of Pavlov's dogs who were rewarded for successfully differentiating between an ellipse and a circle; as the experimenters gradually shaped the ellipses into circles and the circles into ellipses, the dogs experienced the impossibility of the task and essentially went mad. This is how some people describe their working conditions now.

At the same time as such conditions of precariousness, uncertainty and stressful anxiety become the norm for a very large section of our working population (including the top managers) there is an escalation in complexity on all fronts which may leave us feeling even more deskilled. As one manager said, 'Even if you don't change, change is being foisted on you'. Continuity is over, and the 'management of change' has in a certain sense become a contradiction in terms. Long-range unpredictability has become the norm and the only constant now is change itself. Well-known organisational consultants are not ashamed to admit as Moult (1990) says, 'We don't know what is happening and we don't know what we are doing.' (p. 177)

We live in an organisational, cultural and scientific world where the old paradigms seem to have lost their usefulness, inspiration and sometimes their values. The nature of change itself, whether through evolutionary development or radical quantum leaps, has changed and it appears that it will only continue changing. The quantity and quality of change itself is changing at the same time as the tempo of change is accelerating. Managers and developers need to enable themselves and empower others to survive these turbulent, unpredictable conditions and transform them into opportunities for survival, if not growth.

Tools for the Kitbag

Invited to speak at the AMED Conference, and faced with this situation, it seemed to me a useful idea to put together what I have found to be the most essential tools for organisational practitioners. I don't think that there is any hope that the old paradigms can see us through (even though they may still be very useful on occasion). I therefore set myself the task of identifying the few most useful things that I could teach or enable in a limited time, which could be of use to managers and developers facing the next century.

I am under no illusion that these ideas are some kind of cure-all, placebo or infallible prescription. Indeed, I think the one single factor which causes the greatest pain as people struggle with these conditions whirling around us towards the end of this century is the Utopian fallacy – the childlike hope in each one of us that someone somewhere should have the answers, or that someone somewhere should come up with a solution which will alleviate, if not obviate, our distress.

The tools are divided here into

- metaphors
- attitudes
- skills
- behaviours

in a reasonably arbitrary way to be used, changed or discarded just the

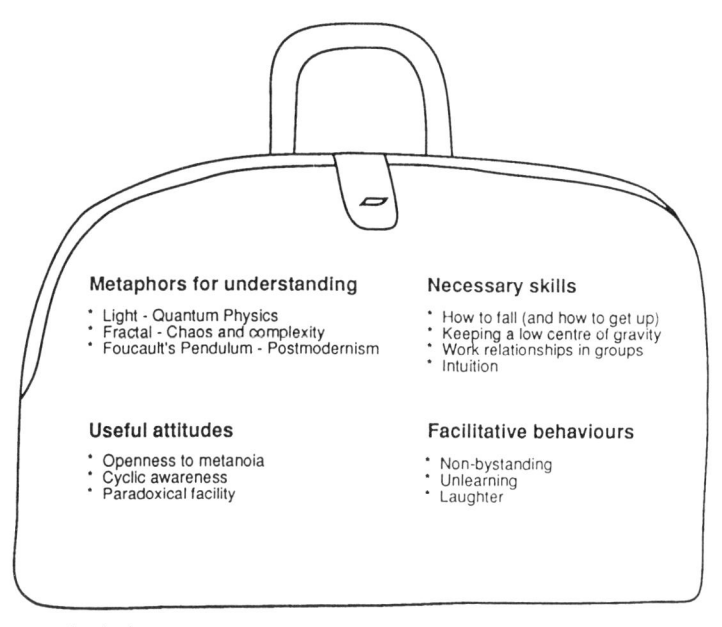

Metaphors for understanding
* Light - Quantum Physics
* Fractal - Chaos and complexity
* Foucault's Pendulum - Postmodernism

Necessary skills
* How to fall (and how to get up)
* Keeping a low centre of gravity
* Work relationships in groups
* Intuition

Useful attitudes
* Openness to metanoia
* Cyclic awareness
* Paradoxical facility

Facilitative behaviours
* Non-bystanding
* Unlearning
* Laughter

Figure 10.1 The kitbag.

way one would equipment in a real kitbag.

Metaphors for Enhancing Understanding

For most of the so-called modern era we have followed scientific, cultural and organisational paradigms based on Newtonian physics, laws of cause and effect, incremental increases in knowledge, the ever upward-pointing arrow of progress. Much of organisational psychology is still firmly wedded to this old model. This does not mean that the old model is not useful, but we are looking for help in contemporary and future conditions.

The first category of tools in any kitbag for the future would therefore be a set of *new metaphors* which may provide us with shapes or intuitive patterns in order to begin to form what are perhaps experimental and attitudinal disciplines as well as to open up avenues for creativity. I believe these comparatively new metaphors have enormously important implications for the training curriculum, managerial development, and as a general response to people's need. They come from fields which few people will ever master, yet they affect each one of us profoundly as persons and as professionals. We can but proceed with fumbling and intuitive steps.

Light

On a quantum group dynamics workshop Professor Isham quoted Niels Bohr: 'If you are not shocked by quantum physics, you have not understood what is going on'. Although light is only one example, it is here meant to be the symbolic representation of an enormously complex and disturbing field. The implications of quantum physics for organisational and management psychology are potentially enormous, but I will briefly point out four examples.

Waves on Mondays, Wednesday and Fridays

One of the first lessons of quantum physics is that apparently contradictory views of reality co-exist. For example, in the words of Sir William Bragg, 'Elementary particles seem to be waves on Mondays, Wednesdays and Fridays and particles on Tuesdays, Thursdays and Saturdays' (Koestler, 1972, p. 52). This metaphor invites the willingness to deal with simultaneous contradiction in the physical as well as the psychological and organisational world.

The observer is always part of the field

The second example concerns the notion that the observer is always part of the field and that, therefore, ultimately all our so-called 'knowledge' is profoundly and ineradicably relative. The new physics makes it untenable to consider an objective or value-free scientific approach, or the idea that a consultant can be 'objective' or 'neutral'. For example, it requires us to take on board fully the notion that there is nothing we can discuss or consider in isolation from ourselves or, for that matter, from the entire environment surrounding us.

We are never separate from others

The new physics also underlines the vitality of the relationship field, which can be explored through the idea of 'state entanglement'. The importance and different natures of relationship in organisations is further explored in Chapter 6.

> The closer we analyse some 'thing' the less it appears as a thing and the more it appears as a dynamic process (things in relationship). Consequently, relationships become a primary source of our knowledge of the world. This can be taken to the ontological extreme by stating that things do not exist ... that, in fact, things ultimately are relationships (Cottone, 1988, p. 360).

We'll never know for sure

The next, vital aspect of quantum physics as it relates to organisational work which I find particularly helpful is Heisenberg's (1930) *uncertainty principle*. For managers and for teachers of management and organisational behaviours, this implies that there are some things, no matter how accurate our apparatus or calibration, that we cannot ever know for certain. I do not believe that study of the organisational implications of this should devolve into some kind of sloppy, 'anything goes' attitude. Of course there is much that we do know and can know. It is more to do with acknowledging and valuing the inherent and intrinsic indeterminacy of human and organisational phenomena, thus challenging our hubris at the same time as extending our compassion for our inevitable shortfall from perfection.

A fractal

'Fractal geometry describes the tracks and marks left by the passage of dynamical activity' (Briggs, 1992, p. 22). The word 'fractal' was coined by Mandelbrot (1974) to describe the phenomenon of a repeating pattern – elements of the whole are repeated in every fragment, and spiral off each other towards creative evolution. Just as the galaxy pulsates, so too does nerve tissue. The same is true for the human heart – and so too, surely, for the organisation. The evocative images of fractals have become icons for the new science of Chaos.

Chaos rules OK

> The first Chaos theorists ... had an eye for pattern, especially pattern that appeared on different scales at the same time. They had a taste for randomness and complexity, for jagged edges and sudden leaps... They feel that they are turning back a trend in science toward reductionism, the analysis of systems in terms of their constituent parts ... they believe that they are looking for the whole. (Gleick, 1989, p. 5)

Chaos concerns the pattern within randomness as an aspect of complexity (Waldrop, 1992). Chaos sometimes convulses dynamic systems and sometimes simply resides in the background. From chaos often comes a new, more complex and differentiated order. Chaos has often been used as a negative word: sometimes chaos is a sign of incompetence, and the description of an organisation or teamwork as 'chaotic' has been a term of disapprobation. However, chaos theory offers us a new meaning and a new way of looking at options for responding to chaotic conditions: not with an expectation of disintegration or panic at the lack of structure, but an openness to the emergence of novel and more creative outputs.

Stability kills

The fractal stimulates; stability kills. Given the very complex and challenging economic and organisational conditions in which we live at the moment, creativity is required more than ever. Though creativity and balance are arch-enemies, they are essential to one another (see Zohar 1990 on quantum relationships). The literature of chaos normalises and values imbalances. Creativity happens at far-from-equilibrium conditions (Gruber, 1988); it often needs the stimulus of deadlines, emotional turmoil or a change of setting to flourish.

The corollary may be that stability sometimes kills; balance leads to stagnation and 'the middle way' is a state often achieved just before disintegration and death. Chaos scientists have discovered that predictability and regularity can be a sign of illness – the only time the heartbeat is completely regular, for example, is shortly before a coronary. The healthy organism, and therefore the healthy organisation, is always out of balance and this process of flux is an intrinsic part of natural processes: the flexibility, the innovation, the capacity for finding novel solutions in changing conditions.

Wholeness

Chaos theorists have a preoccupation with wholeness. This preoccupation has of course existed since the beginning of time. It is a modern phenomenon to try to reduce things to their constituent parts. However, the search for wholeness is now being taken very seriously. For example, Briggs and Peat (1990) state:

> The whole shape of things depends on the most minute part. The part is the whole in this respect, for through the action of any part, the whole in the form of chaos or transformative change may manifest. (p. 75)

This has peculiar, even amazing implications for organisational work – perhaps any segment of an organisation, however unrepresentative or unrelated it may appear, encodes the whole of the organisation. An intervention into any fractal of an organisation in this sense would be an intervention into the whole of the organisation, and may possess the solution for the whole. It is possible that our current limitations of habit and theory can evolve to take on the radically new possibilities which open up to organisational consultants and managers when we take this gestalt seriously into our practice.

Imputed leadership

If we follow the idea of wholeness from chaos theory and begin to apply it to what we know about organisations, I think it has the greatest implications in terms of leadership. If the individual cannot be separated from his or her group context or organisational field, from the dynamic ebb and flow of organisational life and development, then it follows that there is no genuine separation or difference from leadership and the group.

Leadership may be a hidden factor in the nature of the so-called 'strange attractor', the existence of which can but be imputed. As such, it is not directly identified or seen. The function of leadership can lie not in what you do but the way in which you disturb the field. Perhaps the most effective leaders create turbulent space within which they can act as an inferred attractor, from which a pattern can be discovered and form can develop. It is possible that as soon as the form rigidifies, when they stop causing turbulence in the field, they are no longer functional. A leader who is no longer maintaining him- or herself in disequilibrium may be part of an organisation in decay, like a pile of leaves.

Butterfly effect

One of the other most disturbing discoveries is that small events can cause very large effects, and large events may lead to only very small effects. Unfortunately, we do not always know when these conditions apply, but we do know that they sometimes do. This dependence upon initial conditions is known in science as the 'butterfly effect': the idea that a butterfly stirring its wings in China can cause major storms in America. This notion must make the work of organisational consultants exceptionally difficult, particularly when they try to attribute changes to their intervention. However, it does mean that perhaps even small inputs into our world may have profound results.

Foucault's Pendulum – the postmodernist change

The title of Umberto Eco's novel is included in this symbolic kitbag as a symbol or metaphor for a postmodernist view of the world. Postmodernism is defined in contradistinction to modernism. Modernism was characterised by a search for an ultimate truth, a belief in incremental progressions in knowledge and clear boundaries between different disciplines; in effect a master text, such as Freud or Marx once provided (Adair, 1993).

No more heroes: No more 'one truth'

Postmodernism is characterised by 'a diversity of purpose, a confusion of boundaries and an eclecticism' (Moult, 1990, p. 173). New technology and discoveries have meant that we have more realities to contend with. A new, more complex, technological language has proliferated with which we seek to explain it all, but fail repeatedly. We have seen ideological dream after ideological dream flower and fail to solve the monumental problems facing our world: the impending destruction of the planet, the millions of people dying of hunger and disease, and the rise of religious or political fundamentalism to a disturbing degree.

> We live in a world in which the authority of previous guides has apparently crumbled. They have become fragments, bits of a particular archive (of Western Europe, of the white male voice), part of a local history that once involved the presumption (and power) to speak in the name of the world (Chambers, 1990, p. 81)

Many more stories

There is now a disillusion with the metanarrative, the grand answers, the next organisational development fad; and yet we cannot afford the luxury of despair (like the fashionable nihilism of the 1960s) because of the painful economic and cultural conditions which impinge upon us daily – if not personally, then through our newspapers and television. In a culture of multiple narratives, many stories are true, and there is no longer one story.

> For sense here lies not in the separate fates of individualised identities and isolated accounts, but in the interconnected weaving together of the stories, languages, differences and bodies in which we are caught. (Chambers, 1990, p. 10)

We are all responsible

This kind of consciousness leads inevitably to an awareness of values and collective issues, and mandates engaged participation where everybody is responsible for the 'whole thing' because we can no longer hide from the knowledge of it all. 'There is no promise of utopias here, but the possibility of active and engaged participation in cultural process is significantly enhanced' (Gergen, 1990, p. 33).

Useful attitudes

Alongside these metaphors I have also packed three attitudes which help to empower us in the face of an uncertain future.

Openness to metanoia

A useful concept is that of *metanoia*. It is similar in effect to the flipover effect in chaos theory. For Laing and Esterson (1972), metanoia is 'dialectical rationality, a praxis of reconciliation and dynamic unity, an enterprise of continual and continuing reappraisal and renewal, constantly bringing forth new experience with deepening understanding and wholeness' (p. 63). Metanoia is a turnaround, a change of heart that can only happen in openness to change and the disorientation it may bring. Therefore we may need a positive attitude to change, an investment in evolution, and the willingness to bear the disintegrating and fragmenting forces without incapacitating ourselves. Implicit in the process of metanoia as viewed from a gestalt perspective is the reversal of figure and ground. This kind of sharp change occurs when we refocus on the same presented realities but with a completely reversed emphasis. For instance, when looking at a picture, we can concentrate on the shapes created by the positive forms, or on the shapes created by the spaces between – the negative shapes.

Cyclic awareness – what goes around comes around

The next important attitude is a cyclic awareness. This manifests in the willingness to do something again and again, knowing that the nature of change experience is cyclic (or resembles a spiral). Apparently, we need to enter the void again and again if we are to emerge more fully and completely. In a sense we can say that linearity has reached the end of the line. The new era requires that we bring back the right hemisphere of the brain (the non-verbal side of us that works in flashes of images rather than in words) which is our source of creativity, of lateral thinking, of intuition and linking leaps of faith. We may see even leaders who take an evolutionary rather than revolutionary role.

Heraclitus, whose wisdom has endured since 500 BC, postulated that the only thing in life of which we can be sure, is change. Furthermore, the nature of change is cyclical. Everything is in a constant state of flux, and human experience is continuously trying to make meaning from the ever-recurring cyclic interplay between things staying the same and things changing.

Paradoxical facility – the end of causality

Unknowability and uncertainty of many 'facts' means the end of causality and long-range predictability. However, we may not yet have equivalently useful conceptual or experiential structures to replace and/or augment the old notions of linear and sequential causality. Any working kitbag must contain the belief that the past is past, consistency is flawed, and, more often than not, contradiction is in. This necessitates a positive attitude to change and an investment in personal experience of change, particularly during 'the dark night of the soul', which seems to be an essential requirement for any creative breakthrough, whether in art, organisations, psychotherapy or international change. It has become necessary to be comfortable with paradox.

Necessary Skills

Here follows a brief list of skills which, when added to the metaphors in the kitbag, may equip us to cope better with the changing circumstances – systemic, societal, and individual – in which we find ourselves.

How to fall (and how to get up)

'Rolling with the punches' is another way of expressing a willingness to enter the fray, or maybe to enter the void, and to try to survive through flexibility and spontaneity, knowing that you influence the system as much as it influences you. Flexibility in this sense includes the willingness to feel our emotions of love, grief, anger, joy, rather than to suppress or deny them. The skill of falling and getting up, of surrender and yielding again and again includes knowing how to make mistakes and admit defeat – and 'start all over again'. Pseudocompetency or the Achilles syndrome occurs when pretence or covering up substitutes for true competence and confidence (Clarkson, 1993).

How to keep your centre of gravity low

This skill concerns the psychological and physical ability to mobilise in any direction, like a tennis player preparing to return serve. A high and unstable centre of gravity is associated with a person who gives out more than they take in. Empathic listening is therefore an essential low gravity habit. Staying close to the ground is another.

How to work relationships in groups

This will be a vital skill if we are all to pool our resources in a living example of dynamic interrelatedness. As it becomes increasingly clear that the old paradigms are outdated, even the way groups operate may also be in flux. The classical model of groups was a deterministic one, defined in stages and generally model-oriented. Basic assumptions were made about the group, and so its process and eventual outcome could be anticipated. Now, however, we are more aware that groups are probabilistic rather than deterministic; they are not based on cause and effect, and therefore have an uncertain outcome. We see that any group creates itself through its own dynamic process, with the observer specifying the process at the point of definition. Patterns emerge from the group which, like fractals, hold all the potential of the group, for all things are related and nothing exists in isolation. See Table 10.1.

Intuition

Successful entrepreneurs are often highly intuitive personality types. The development of innovative strategy is often based on intuition rather than the linear logic of old-style planning. A 'radar' system is needed that is the result partly of relevant experience, partly wise reflection and partly inspired guesswork. This radar system needs to operate in a trusted way in order for it to work quickly enough to be useful in fast-changing situations.

Facilitative Behaviours

No kitbag for the future, no matter how small, would be complete without the following helpful behaviours.

Non-bystanding

A bystander is considered to be a person who does not become actively involved in a situation where someone else requires help. Where one or more people are in danger, bystanders therefore could, by taking some form of action, affect the outcome of the situation even if they are not able to avert it (Clarkson, 1992) (see Chapter 11).

In today's turbulent world, it is neither ethical nor practical to maintain that things are not our business, or to deny that we influence outcomes. Nor is it enough to espouse values without enacting them; righteous indignation becomes rather empty when devoid of action. It is the difference between what is called on the street 'talking the talk' and 'walking the walk'.

Unlearning

There is a fashionable pre-occupation with the learning organisation these days. However, I think that the unlearning organisation is at least equally important – sometimes bridges must be burnt. It is the extent to which we hang on to old habits that prevents us from recognising that previously effective solutions have now become problems in themselves and inhibit our capabilities. We must of course always remember that any solution will contain the seeds of future problems. In counselling as in organisational consultancy, there is a lot of work to be done around letting go of the old – old belief systems and old hierarchies – and not

Table 10.1 Quantum group dynamics: a comparative table (Clarkson and Clayton, 1992)

	New group process	**Classical group process**
Self-creating group	Group creates itself through its dynamic process The observer specifies the process at the point of definition.	Defined in stages; generally model oriented
Relatedness and fractals	Patterns emerge from the group which hold all the potential of the group All things are related, nothing exists in isolation	Basic assumptions made are about the group
	Acknowledged that the group leader affects the group process, they are a whole system	Group leader often seen as separate from the group
Entanglement	The influence of members of the group on each other is an integral part of the process, both during the group time and continuing beyond, throughout life	The influence of members in the group on each other is recognised during the group meeting but not as a continuing influence once the group have parted
Probabilities	Outcome is uncertain and unpredictable, not based on cause and effect Probabilistic	Process and outcome predetermined with some certainty and predictability Deterministic
	The group works holistically and existentially, therefore acknowledges the influence of the past and future on the present state	Work with the past, the future and sometimes existentially
	The leader of the group has an influence on the group despite independence of the group	Leadership issues are mainly around dependency/ independence
Measurement	The measure is only that of an instant ... the world is dynamic and moves on The observer defines the measurement, the measurement creates the reality	The measure (of 'success') is absolute The reality is there to be measured.
	Differences between members of the group emerge through contact within the group, no deliberate assumptions made about roles, the group are constantly open to change	Assumptions are often made about personal attributes and the different roles individual members of the group perform (i.e. Belbin). These can become self-fulfilling!

maintaining traditionalism just for its own self-perpetuating sake, or because the old way is perceived as being too difficult or costly to change.

Laughter – the cosmic giggle

Humour is acknowledged in folk wisdom as one of the best natural medicines, and maintaining the capacity to find humour in life situations is a life-preserving and life-enhancing skill. Abraham Lincoln was criticised for making jokes during the American Civil War strategy meetings, but he replied, 'If I couldn't have these 20-second breaks, the horror of the situation would kill me'. It is not to deny the seriousness of our situation, but if we take the real issues seriously enough we can free ourselves to laugh as well, to see things in perspective and to find hope and courage even in the midst of the worst despair.

Temporary Conclusion

I want to end on a quote of an unknown author from whom I have remembered the following line: 'I must warn you against the unfortunate use of what I have to say'. I do know that all of these notions can be abused, misunderstood and used out of context. I also believe these embryonic ideas can be helpful in developing training, managers, organisational consultancy, personal counselling and national responses to people in need in the current conditions. I hope they serve you well and that you will add freely to them forever.

Acknowledgements

Grateful thanks to Patricia Shaw, Geoff Mead, Vincent Keyter and Denton Roberts for their help in shaping this material for publication as well as to Rita Cremona for the kitbag illustration.

References

Adair, G. (1993). 'Scrutiny: Freud slips into the shadows', *Sunday Times*, 9 May, London.
Briggs, J. (1992). *Fractals: The Patterns of Chaos*. London: Thames and Hudson.
Briggs, J. and Peat, F. D. (1990). *Turbulent Mirror*. New York: Harper & Row
Chambers, I. (1990). *Border Dialogues: Journeys in Postmodernity*. London: Routledge.
Clarkson, P. (1992). *Transactional Analysis Psychotherapy: An Integrated Approach*. London: Routledge.
Clarkson, P. (1993). *The Achilles Syndrome*. Cirencester: Element.
Clarkson, P. and Clayton, S. (1992). Quantum Group Dynamics. Unpublished manuscript arising from lecture delivered at Second European Groupwork Symposium, 10 July 1992.

Cottone, R. R. (1988). 'Epistemological and ontological issues in counselling: Implications of social systems theory', *Counselling Psychology Quarterly*, 1(4),357–65

Gergen, K. (1990). 'Towards a postmodern psychology', *The Humanistic Psychologist*, **18**, 23–34

Gleick, J. (1989). *Chaos: Making a New Science*. London:Heinemann.

Gruber, H. (1988). 'Inching our way up Mount Olympus: The evolving systems approach to creative thinking'. In *The Nature of Creativity* (Robert J. Sternberg, Ed.). Cambridge: Cambridge University Press.

Heisenberg, W. (1930). *The Physical Principles of the Quantum Theory*. New York: Dover.

Koestler, A. (1972). *The Roots of Coincidence*. London: Hutchinson.

Laing, R. D. and Esterson, A. (1972). *Leaves of Spring*. Harmondsworth: Penguin.

Mandelbrot, B. B. (1974). *The Fractal Geometry of Nature*. New York: Freeman.

Moult, G. (1990). 'Under new management', *MEAD* **21**(3), 171–82

Waldrop, M. M. (1992). *Complexity: The Emerging Science at the Edge of Order and Chaos*. Harmondsworth: Penguin.

Zohar, D. (1990). *The Quantum Self*. London: Bloomsbury.

Chapter 11
Bystanding in organisations

A block to empowerment

PETRŪSKA CLARKSON and PATRICIA SHAW

The Problem

Sometimes there is an injustice, a cruelty or a victimisation of one or more people in the organisation and people turn away saying 'it has nothing to do with me'. Sometimes consultants work in organisations where the ethics may be very different from their own. Sometimes the idea of the bystander from social psychology can be very useful in finding ways of taking responsibility for collective behaviour. It can even be very empowering to do so. I am told it may also be disturbing to the status quo.

Introduction

At a management team meeting a decision needs to be made about a difficult issue for which there are no easy solutions. After some debate, and pushing by the formal leader, a decision is apparently agreed. Several participants are aware that they have not expressed in this forum views, doubts and suggestions relating to the implications of this decision which they have privately discussed with one another and with others outside the meeting. The formal leader will be held accountable for this decision at the next level above in the organisation. In holding their peace, several team members have not offered assistance in a critical situation. When asked later they give a variety of explanations and rationales for their behaviour, most of which probably fall into one of the categories listed above.

Bystanding

This kind of activity (or non-activity) has been identified as bystanding. (The term was born from an incident in New York where a young woman was murdered within sight and earshot of dozens of people, who all avoided doing something about it.) A bystander is thus someone who does not become actively involved in a situation in which others require assistance of some kind. Bystanding is the nemesis of organisational empowerment. It may give temporary relief from responsibility at one level, but at another level not.

When an organisation has espoused empowerment as a desired characteristic, it is tempting for all the discussion to be focused on trying to reach joint understanding of the meaning and concrete implications of this much used term. It seems to us fruitful for people to have ways to understanding and recognising some of the dynamics of disempowerment. Our thesis is that it is not only the central players in any situation, nor only those with formal authority, not abstractions such as management, who can significantly influence events, but that the *most potent possibilities of change in many organisations lie with those who would disclaim such power – the bystanders.*

Bystanding behaviour meets the following criteria:

- People are aware that something seems wrong in a situation.
- They do not actively take responsibility for their part in maintaining the problem – preventing its resolution.
- They claim they could not have acted otherwise.
- They are discounting their autonomy and power to influence the situation.

Bystander phrases

There are many ways of adopting the bystander role in professional and organisational life. Below we identify a dozen examples we have come to recognise. Any one organisational culture will tend to support some examples in particular. The behaviour is both a manifestation of the organisation culture and is continually recreating that culture. Each example is characterised by a typical phrase which a 'bystander' might use to account for their behaviour.

'It's none of my business'

Here there is a conflict or difficult situation and a person, on the basis of not being a central player, discounts any responsibility for influencing the events, when they could mediate, ask someone else to mediate, express their views, give information, and so on.

'This situation is more complex than it seems'

The person uses the complexity and variety of real life situations to justify non-involvement, rather than helping to clarify the situation or saying, in effect, 'I don't understand all that is going on here, but from what I appreciate so far...'

'I do not have the all the information/ am not qualified to deal with this'

Rarely does anyone have all the information about any situation before they are called upon to act, indeed the very absence of information may underline the need for action. To refuse to bystand may be to accept that 'What I do know is useful and what I don't know I can begin to find out or find out why I can't find out.'

'I don't want to get burned again'

Someone refuses involvement because a past intervention was not effective or had negative results: 'Last time I tried to speak to X he shouted at me'. Instead they could reflect on and learn from the previous encounter something about effective intervention, which they experiment with now instead of withdrawing to safety.

'I want to remain neutral'

Here someone masks their failure to decide what to do by appearing to be invested in fairness and a supposedly higher moral ground. However, neutrality always favours the aggressor. It is *possible* to be interested in all the grievances people have, to be on both or all sides and to actively support everyone, or to realise that the desire to be fair to all sides may include the necessity of pointing out where one side may be being unfair.

'I'm only telling the truth (to others) as I see it'

A person jumps to conclusions and takes every opportunity to tell their version of the truth to others without checking their perceptions with, challenging, or seeking to understand the parties directly involved. They thus exchange a contribution to collective problem solving for the popularity of the carrier of juicy gossip.

'I'm just following orders'

A person claims they are unable to act autonomously in a situation because they are subject to higher authority or popular demand. Convenient obedience to persons or rigid bureaucratic procedures is meant to guarantee personal exoneration while allowing blaming of 'them' or the rules. The possibilities of protest or creative bending of the rules to meet the challenge of the situation are denied.

'I expect it's six of one and half a dozen of the other'

The jury concludes that the truth lies somewhere in the middle. Truth is so relative that responsibility can be abrogated.

'My contribution won't make much difference'

The politics and power of the organisation are believed to be too great for an individual to have any influence at all. A person does not deny that there is a contribution to be made, but that theirs is so insignificant as to be worthless. Instead they could join forces with others and pool resources.

'I'm simply keeping my own counsel'

Unless the person believes their own interests are threatened they do not get involved. There is a failure to acknowledge that part of taking care of yourself involves taking care of others. Everybody benefits from a more caring situation.

'They brought it on themselves'

A person justifies their non-involvement on the grounds that if something has gone wrong the key figures probably deserved it, and it behoves the audience to stay out of the way of their just retribution.

'I dont want to rock the boat'

By avoiding conflict and confrontation in the name of political wisdom, this person ignores the fact that any disturbing dynamic will eventually emerge and take effect anyway. Instead they need to find a way of expressing their concerns even if they seem to be starting a disturbance, and then to remain committed to an effective resolution of such a disturbance, while the storm rages. Another name for this is 'victim-blaming'

What To Do About It?

We are not advocating meddling or interfering at every single opportunity or leaping in to 'rescue' those who do not in fact need assistance. We are suggesting that it is important to realise that, in any situation about which you have knowledge or with which you are in contact, necessarily means you are already involved. As we know from modern physics all observers are part of the field and even the act of observation affects what is observed.

The last of human freedoms Frankl defines so vividly and poignantly as the freedom to choose one's attitude in any given set of circumstances, even Auschwitz and Dachau. 'Every day, every hour, offered the opportunity to make a decision, a decision which determined whether you would or would not submit to those powers which threatened to rob you of your very self, your inner freedom; which determined whether or not you would become moulded into the form of the typical inmate' (Frankl, 1969, pp. 65–6). Modern-day organisations can also limit external choices, but definitely not as much as those.

The question becomes 'What is the best way to be involved?' and does not always mean doing something directly or immediately. Understanding and accepting personal responsibility for bystanding behaviour may be uncomfortable. There is a deep heritage in many organisations of covering your own back, turning a blind eye, allowing or enjoying scapegoating and relishing the vicarious excitement of office politics. One important lesson is not to wait to see which way the wind is blowing, but to make choices while the story is still unfolding, to decide how to be and do before the scene is played out and while the result remains ambiguous.

In collusively bystanding cultures, which tend to flourish in bureaucratic organisations, the advantages of such a position can seem minimal – the penalties of having 'backed the wrong horse', criticism, isolation, a black note on the file, or dwindling career prospects.

So what *are* the possible advantages? At a personal level, the satisfaction of expressing one's energy in the service of integrity and responsibility rather than turning it inwards into sleepless nights, gnawing doubts, ulcers and heart disease. Also exchanging the vitality of engaging in a struggle for what you believe to be right, rather than the vicarious excitement of political gossip. There are also fertile opportunities for learning and increasing one's knowledge of how to be effective amongst the complexities of organisational life. This is at least one way of understanding the challenge that the call for an empowered organisational culture represents.

Bystanding will always be with us. Organisational or national cultures which support bystanding are essentially disempowering. Individuals can and need to take responsibility for questioning and involving themselves in social justice – wherever it may be needed. There are always consequences (nothing is free); but the individual, collective and organisational health is enhanced when people feel and exercise their freedom to the benefit of all. Bystanding is futher explored in Clarkson (1995).

References

Clarkson, P. (1995). *The Bystander*. London: Routledge.
Frankl, V. (1969) *Man's Search for Meaning*. London: Hodder and Stoughton.

Chapter 12
2500 years of gestalt

From Heraclitus to the Big Bang

PETRŪSKA CLARKSON

The Problem

The nature and level of individual and organisational stress and distress are experienced in many different countries as we attempt to be effective in current world conditions. This material was originally developed for people who spoke 'Gestalt'. The themes are eternal and universal.

Introduction

This chapter suggests that there are three themes which, although they overlap and interact themselves as wholes, between them embrace the most important emphases in gestalt. These are:

- everything is a whole
- everything changes
- everything is related to everything else.

These themes are traced from their earliest source in the Western tradition – Heraclitus – through Smuts and Perls to the constantly changing frontiers of scientific enquiry, such as quantum physics and chaos theory. It is suggested that these sources (the most ancient and the most modern) are to be counted, acknowledged and used as theoretical works in the gestalt canon with great implication for conceptualisation, method, attitude and technique. These applications may be to individual or organisational work.

Gestalt therapy has suffered from a dearth of theoretical and clinical publications. At the same time it has established itself in experiential and practical applications throughout the world. In some European countries, for example Holland, I believe that gestalt has had some difficulty being accepted as an independent psychotherapy because of what was perceived as 'a lack of theory'. I don't know who made the submissions, but it certainly is not my impression that there is a lack of theoretical works on, or about, the central concerns of gestalt.

One way in which some gestalt practitioners, theoreticians and teachers have tried to resolve this felt lack is by bringing in – through importation, introjection or integration – concepts, ideas and theories from other fields and other disciplines. These are often far removed from both the philosophical and cultural core of gestalt; thus, in my opinion, impugning the integrity of the gestalt approach. This tendency is exemplified in what someone has called the 'gestalt and ..' syndrome – gestalt and bodywork, gestalt and aromatherapy, gestalt and self-psychogy, gestalt and object relations, as if gestaltists do not have or cannot develop theory and methodology sufficient from what already exists in gestalt. It is as if such large-scale and sometimes wise, sometimes indiscriminate borrowing from other universes of discourse or other approaches, can become a cheap and easy way to expand the gestalt corpus.

However, I have very serious doubts about this procedure as a way of enhancing gestalt. Furthermore, I do not believe it is necessary, because I think that there is a very large number of books, sources, theories and approaches which share the central philosophical and methodological tenets of gestalt. These need to be recognised as gestalt textbooks, since they belong inside the cadre of gestalt more than anywhere else. I am thinking, for example, of the work of the phenomenologists such as Merleau-Ponty in *The Phenomenology of Perception* (1970) and Minkowski in *Temps Vecu* (Lived Time) (1970). But an extensive discussion of these must wait for another time. For our purposes here, I wish particularly to reclaim two sets of textbooks or theoretical works which I believe to be more truly gestalt than anything else. I believe they are amongst our most important gestalt source books. The continuity of a tradition of 2500 years spans gestalt thinking from the beginning of time in the Western tradition, to the current frontiers of the scientific enquiry of our current world. Between them they seem to me to constitute a whole contact cycle, from the ancient pre-Socratic texts of Heraclitus over to the modern interpreters of quantum physics and chaos theory such as Capra (1978), Zohar (1990), Bohm (1983), Gleick (1989) and Briggs and Peat (1989). They reach of course, far beyond Gestalt.

I will take up this idea of a continuity of gestalt preoccupations in terms of three themes. This is to show the continuous line of certain themes of consciousness through from the pre-Socratic philosophies using Perls *et al.* (1951) as the central textbook in our discipline, through the developing areas in our modern sciences, to the most modern of scientific developments. These three themes are

- everything is a whole
- everything changes
- everything is related to everything else.

Of course they could be phrased somewhat differently – they interrelate and, between them form an ever-changing dynamically interconnected whole. The three major themes are formulated here in three very simple sentences. As I refer to each theme, please realise that these ideas are themselves in the process of development and may very well change, even in the course of this enunciation. And if the themes that I point out may seem simple, it absolutely does not mean that they are simplistic.

I can do no more here than indicate in the briefest of examples some directions in which I have been thinking, working and writing. I hope that in doing so I can encourage you to do likewise. I think that the connotational fields which they draw into their wake are extremely rich, and could possibly encompass all of gestalt theory and practice. Indeed, I have been very committedly playing with the idea that all of gestalt theory and practice could be taught from extrapolating these three themes alone.

My thesis is that gestalt as a psychotherapeutic and organisational approach would hardly be discomfited by, and perhaps compatible with, the radical revisions and assumptions of the paradox-embracing climate with which we are confronted on our conceptual and experiential horizons of our time. Workshops at Physis, where we work with the theoretical and practical implications of such modern developments (for example quantum group dynamics in organisations), have attracted great interest.

Holism or Everything is a Whole

The first major theme that seems to run as a continuous thread of gestalt consciousness from the most ancient to the most present time, is the idea of holism – the notion that everything is a whole. This notion I trace to Heraclitus, whom I have come to accept as the original grandfather of gestalt. Heraclitus was a Greek philosopher of Ephesus who lived from 'about 536–470 BC' (Runes, 1966, p. 124). Throughout the Heraclitean canon we find many and varied statements and restatements of the idea that everything is essentially a whole or a gestalt. To take one example:

Connections
wholes and not wholes (= parts)
convergent divergent
consonant dissonant
out of all a one
and out of a one all. (Heraclitus in Guerrière, 1980, pp. 94–5)

A meditation on the meaning and implications of this fragment tends to invite us into feeling how profoundly Heraclitus understood and wanted to communicate the intrinsic one-ness of all phenomena. He can be seen as one of the first holists in the Western tradition. Nowadays, holism is defined as:

> The theory that the fundamental principle of the universe is the creation of wholes, i.e. complete and self-contained systems from the atom and the cell by evolution to the most complex forms of life and mind: the theory that a complex entity, system etc. is more than merely the sum of its parts. (Schwartz *et al.*, 1988, p. 678)

The experiential exercise suggested here is in the form of an experiment. People pair up and then take the most anonymous object that they have on their person – the object or article which is least likely to contain anything personal to them, for example an article of clothing like a sock. Then, in the usual gestalt way, they each then spend some minutes speaking in turn to their partner, speaking as that item or article. At the end of the exercise, people are asked to experiment with saying this sentence: 'And this is my existence', to experience the idea that the identification with such an apparently anonymous article can come to represent the nature of the whole. If you pull on the fragment, as with a thread on a jersey, it often encompasses the wholeness of the person – at least for that moment. For many people this indeed was their experience in the experiment. Even through identification with an apparently innocuous part object, they discovered some essence of their existence as a whole, as a personality, or as an existent. What some workshop participants found particularly fascinating was that the smaller the detail, the more particular, the more representative of the whole it became.

> Now what is first to be considered is that the organism always works as a whole. We *have* not a liver or a heart. We *are* liver and heart and brain and so on, and even this is wrong. We are not a summation of parts, but a *coordination* – a very subtle coordination of all these different bits that go into the making of the organism. The old philosophy always thought that the world consisted of the sum of particles. You know yourself it's not true. We consist originally out of one cell. (Perls, 1969b, p. 5)

The concept of holism is probably the most central feature of gestalt psychology and gestalt psychotherapy. Of course gestalt psychology is based on the concept that the whole is based on the total configuration or that the whole is more than the sum of its parts. Therefore, any part can be said to encode the whole. Perls *et al.* (1951) give a useful definition of gestalt: 'Configuration, structure, theme, structural relationship (Korzybski) or meaningful organized whole most closely approximate the originally German word *Gestalt* ...' (p. ix).

It is also the philosophy espoused and developed by one of the major unrecognised influences on gestalt, namely Jan Smuts, the South African philosopher-General who was an originator of the League of Nations, which became the United Nations. Smuts' ideas were the dominant, and perhaps one of the only, philosophical and intellectually interesting cultural influences in South Africa at the time that Perls was there with Laura, forming the first foundation stones of gestalt and writing *Ego, Hunger and Aggression* (1969a). We know that Perls visited Smuts at his estate at Irene near Pretoria, and elsewhere (Clarkson and Mackewn, 1993) I have drawn attention to how even the origins of the gestalt cycle can be found in Smuts' major work, *Holism and Evolution* (1987). Here follows a representative quotation from Smuts on holism:

> The final net result is that this is a whole-making universe, that it is the fundamental character of this universe to be active in the production of wholes, of ever more complete and advanced wholes, and that the Evolution of the universe, inorganic and organic, is nothing but the record of this whole-making activity in its progressive development (Smuts, 1987, p. 326).

In the introduction to *Gestalt Therapy* (1951), Perls *et al.* emphasise how important it is to heal the dualism in ourselves and in society, and to find the wholeness which is intrinsic to gestalt and to life. Further on, they express this as:

> ... Awareness is only possible of a whole-and-parts, where each part is immediately experienced as involving all the other parts and the whole, and the whole is just of these parts. The whole figure could be said to be the background for the parts, but it is more than ground for it; it is at the same time the figure of the parts, and they are ground. (p. 416)

Also in the modern sciences such as chaos theory, we find similar themes emphasising the presence of the whole in the part, which in a certain sense corroborates the gestalt emphasis on the whole. It also gives a new and modern articulation to the original Heraclitean ideas. For example, Briggs and Peat (1989) state:

> The whole shape of things depends upon the most minute part. The part is the whole in this respect, for through the action of any part, the whole in the form of chaos or transformative change may manifest (p. 75).

Of course, Bohm also has written extensively on the way in which any part encodes the whole (1983). Also:

> Pribram's studies in brain memory and functioning led him to the conclusion that the brain operates, in many ways, like a hologram ... The part is in the whole and the whole is in each part – a type of unity-in-diversity and diversity-in-unity. The key point is simply that the part has access to the whole. (Wilber, 1982, p. 2)

These ideas have important implications for psychotherapy; for example, scientific research such as that in clinical psychology is frequently based on the idea of the representative sample. If we take seriously the concept that any part is in fact fully representative of the whole, it would be impossible to find a non-representative sample of anything. This is because it would only depend on the skilfulness of the observer or worker in order to find the entire whole fully present in the particularity of that moment. There are many examples, but I only have space for one: the way in which people in a group sometimes say that the way they behave in the group or in the individual session is quite different from the way they are anywhere else. From this perspective, whether defended or concealed, whatever part or particularity is present, the whole is enfolded in that fragment in the same way as a fractal of any object enfolds the whole.

The *fractal* – a concept from chaos theory – is an immensely fruitful metaphor to draw upon within gestalt today. The word fractal was coined by Mandelbrot (1974) to describe this phenomenon of a repeating pattern – the whole repeated in every fragment, and thus spiralling off each other towards creative evolution. Perls *et al.* (1951) appeared to have understood this when they wrote:

> But in fact every successive stage is a new whole, operating as a whole, with its own mode of life; it is *its* mode of life, as a concrete whole, that it wants to complete; it is not concerned with seeking 'equilibrium in general'. (p.350)

It has peculiar, and perhaps also amazing, implications for organisational work – perhaps any segment of an organisation, however unrepresentative or unrelated it may appear, encodes the whole of the organisation. An intervention into any fractal of an organisation in this sense would be an intervention into the whole of the organisation. It is possible that our current limitations of habit and theory can evolve to take on radically new possibilities, which open up to organisational consultants and managers when we take this seriously into our practice.

Change, or Everything Changes

To introduce the second theme, which I see as a continuous flow around the cycle of awareness from 500 BC to today, I suggest that people do the experiment of the 'awareness continuum'. It may be familiar to people, and yet my experience is that it can be always new, always bringing forth new awareness, novel avoidances and sometimes spectacular breakthroughs of consciousness. It works by people focusing on completing the sentence 'Now I am aware of ...', 'Now I am aware of ...'. After a few minutes of doing this sincerely and contactfully, most participants report a heightened appreciation of the eternally changing quality of awareness, and therefore of their existence. Whenever we focus fully on any one thing, it tends to move on to the other in an inevitable cyclic pattern. Whenever we fully configure figure, it becomes ground. Vases slip into faces, the background becomes figure. Heraclitus was par excellence the philosopher of change.

> He regarded the universe as a ceaselessly changing conflict of opposites, all things being in a state of flux, coming into being and passing away, and held that fire, the type of this constant change, is their origin. From the passing impressions of experience the mind derives a false idea of the permanence of the external world, which is really in a harmonious process of constant change. (Hawkins and Allen, 1991, p. 663)

So, Heraclitus postulated that change is the only thing in the whole world of which we can be certain. The nature of this change, according to him, is usually cyclic. Perls (1969b) frequently uses the image of not stepping into the same river twice or not pushing the river. I doubt if he was consciously aware of drawing from one of the central metaphors of the Heraclitean legacy:

> Upon those who are (in the process of) stepping
> into the same rivers
> different and again different waters flow.
> (Heraclitus in Guerrière, 1980, p. 104)

The unifying force of all life phenomena which is suggested by Heraclitus is Physis. The river water symbolises the one Physis, or life force. The coincidence of opposite values in one action allows it to be a symbol of the one Physis. Physis was first named by the pre-Socratic Greeks as a generalised creative force of Nature (Guerrière, 1980). It was conceived of as the healing factor in illness, the energetic motive for evolution, and the driving force of creativity in the individual and collective psyche. Physis can be understood to be the life force, and Perls refers to this life force frequently, although not by this name.

> Now, normally the *élan vital*, the life force, energizes by sensing, by listening, by scouting... [it] first mobilises the center.... this basic energy, this life force ... these muscles are used to move about, to take from the world, to touch the world, to be in contact ... (Perls, 1969b, pp. 63–4)

This sense that everything is changing all the time, as the result of contact, is the very heartbeat of the Heraclitean message:

> This order....
> ....always was and is and shall be:
> an ever-living fire, kindling itself in measures and quenching itself in measures. (Heraclitus in Guerrière, 1980, p. 97)

Heraclitus suggests, therefore, that the nature of change is intrinsically rhythmic, kindling and quenching. Any gestaltist is familiar with the rhythms of breathing in and breathing out, of eating and excreting, of arousal and orgasm, of awareness through the stage contact to the stage of withdrawal. This is the intrinsic and inevitable cyclic nature of human existence. What was surprising and delightful to me to discover in Heraclitus was that he even identified the *cyclic nature* of the interplay between stasis and change, homeostatic and dynamic self-regulation, the formation and de-structuring of any whole.

Change or evolution occurs for Heraclitus in a cyclic, patterned rhythm. '*The cycle* is the compact experiential reconciliation of permanence and degeneration. Man exists the cycle or the whole' (Heraclitus in Guerriere, 1980, p. 89). It is clear from this quotation that Heraclitus appreciates the necessity to hold within our experiential reality the notion that structuring and de-structuring is inevitably connected in a *cyclic* configuration. This cycle encapsulates in a metaphorically archetypal form the very nature of the whole of human existence as it exists in a state of ever-recurrent flux.

Of course, as we go to Smuts and to Perls *et al.* we find that the holism we have discussed is a process of creative synthesis. The wholes are not static but evolutionary, creative and in a continual state of flux.

> Elements of both of the actual past and of anticipated future experience are fused with the present experience into one individual act, which as a conscious object of the mind dominates the entire situation with the purview of the purpose or plan. It involves not only *sensations* and *perceptions*, but also concepts of a complex character, *feelings and desires* in respect of the end desired, and volitions in respect of the act intended; which is then put into *action* or *execution* [all italics added]. (Smuts, 1987, p. 158)

The cycle of gestalt formation and destruction has since Heraclitus therefore remained an intrinsic codification of the cyclic nature of the change of human evolutionary wholes. Contrary to some of the ideas in psychoanalysis, which emphasises homeostasis alone, gestalt acknowledges *the need for the living being to create disequilibrium, to strive towards evolutionary or creative change as well, and recognises the de-structuring activity as a necessary part of creative adjustment or creative transformation.*

A similar point is made by Perls *et al.*(1951), in a quotation which again demonstrates how present are Heraclitean concepts in gestalt:

> Given the novelty and the indefinite variety of the environment, no adjustment would be possible, by the conservative inherited self-regulation alone; contact must be a creative transformation. On the other hand, creativity that is not continually destroying and assimilating an environment given in perception and resisting manipulation is useless to the organism and remains

superficial and lacking in energy; it does not become deeply exciting, and it soon languishes (p.406)

Ultimately no organism can survive without assimilating something from the environment or the surrounding field, growing, discharging something into the environment, and then dying. Psychologically and physiologically, this periodic cycle of emergent need (hunger, urge to excrete, to sleep, to compose a symphony) initiates the excitement of the figure/background process; it also attends to the next emergent need of the organism, and progresses the healthy organism towards completion of a particular cycle and the commencement of another one.

The fact of continuous, everlasting change in the physical and psychological universe lies at the heart of everything we are learning in the new physics and chaos theory today. The Heraclitean intuition that flux is all there is, is totally corroborated by most of the modern findings at the front edge of human enquiry. 'Dissipative structures are systems capable of maintaining their identity only by remaining continually open to the flux and flow of their environment' (Briggs and Peat, 1989, p. 139).

Zohar (1990) describes the process thus:

> Quantum field theory takes us even further beyond Newton's dead and silent universe, giving us a vivid picture of the dynamic flux which lies at the heart of an indeterminate being. Here, even those particles which do manifest themselves as individual beings do so only briefly ... [It gives a] graphic picture of the emergence and return, or the beginning and ceasing, of individual subatomic particles at the quantum level of reality [which] holds out deep implications of our way of looking at the nature and function of individual personalities or the survival of the individual self. (p. 13)

One of the many corollaries of appreciating the cyclic nature of phenomena is the importance of the void – the abyss space – which may be fertile or futile according to Perls, but always a recurrent station in this perpetual cyclic motion. It is from the void that the new emerges; it was in the deepest darkness that Moses found God, and it is when we most truly let ourselves go into the emptiness that fullness can begin to arise. The recent scientific thrill of discovering evidence that our known world emerged with a 'big bang' from the void (for example, Davies, 1992) echoes human experience of a sudden insight, a figure/ground shift, a turnaround or enantodromia that obliterates one phenomenological world and brings another into being. Like death, it is inescapable and yet human beings so often try to a-void it. It is my conviction that if we only had time to teach the human race one thing before we self-destruct, it would not be the linear skills of making better products, but rather the cyclic skills of navigating the endless changes in our lives and in our worlds. Furthermore, I consider that the most important of these skills are understanding of the void, along with the skills to transform void experiences into new beginnings again and again and again. I think these are the most valuable lessons now for our planet and particularly for our large systems and nations such as Russia, South Africa, Europe and the many organisations facing progressively unpredictable and increasingly chaotic futures.

Dynamic Interrelatedness, or Everything is Related to Everything Else

The third theme in this '"whole-y" trinity' is process, or dynamic interrelatedness. Colloquially, *everything is related to everything else*. There are potentially many experiments one could do to test this, and I am quite open to the idea that it may not always work. It is possible that people or events may *coincidentally* occur in the same time or space. However, as a gestaltist I am also quite open to the notion that, whenever things occur in the same space at the same time, there is some meaningful relationship between them. Lewin (the conceptual parent of field theory in gestalt) says 'it is no more true in psychology than in physics that "everything depends on everything else" ' (in Perls *et al.*, 1951, p. 277).

I ask the group to stand up and move around the room and after some period of looking at each other, making contact with some or avoiding others, to choose another person and to experiment with discovering whether there was some meaningful connecting or dynamic interrelatedness between them. I have seen this kind of experiment work with astonishing accuracy many times before, and an exact understanding of it is beyond my present capacity. However, I have had experience of one person apparently 'randomly' connecting with another person, both of whom, it turned out, were beaten with wire clothes hangers for being untidy as children. In psychodrama, it has happened that one person who started smoking after an encounter with a rogue elephant matched up with another person who had a similar experience. Such examples of 'tele' from psychodrama (Greenberg, 1975) or synchronicity in Jungian thought (1972) abound, and give credence to the notion that there are meaningfully interconnecting patterns in all of human existence. Repeatedly, many of us exp-erience that, whenever we stop to pay attention to a particular conjunction between events and people, some significance – often profound – is laid bare.

So it seems that the notion that everything is related to everything else is in a sense philosophically, experientially and scientifically accurate. However, we need to understand that this relatedness includes the *opposite* of any particular entity.

Going back to Heraclitus (in Guerrière, 1980): 'Through the one-ness proper to a cycle, the one Physis manifests itself ... *Opposites* may be one in their cycle recurrence: they come around to replace each other' (p. 105). Heraclitus also stresses that: 'Cold phenomena get warm, heat cools down, moisture dries up, the parched gets wet' (p. 105).

Of course, even – or particularly – in Heraclitus, holism, change, and dynamic interrelatedness (even between opposites) are also fractals of *one whole*. By extrapolating three sentences or three aspects, I am merely focusing on three different facets of a unity which intrinsically is indivisible, although it is forever changing, and although its parts are forever interrelated, even as they oppose or contradict each other.

Although Physis is wont to hide itself, it manifests itself in multiple ways. .... The form in which Physis does manifest itself through phenomena is *their one-ness*. That is to say, it suggests a certain one-ness in multiple things, a certain *coincidentia oppositorum* (coincidence of opposites) (Guerrière, 1980, p. 103). All of them suggest the unity of the cosmos.

As we can see, this cosmic unity includes the notion of *enantiodromia*, a term used both by Jung (1968) and by Perls (1969b). This refers to the nature of polarities. Opposites may have contrary qualities, yet they can turn into each other at their apotheosis. The more fully I configure my hate, the more likely that it can turn into love or understanding and of course vice versa. It is unclear whether Perls was conscious or not of the writings of Heraclitus, but he was later to pick up the notion of the dynamic interplay between opposites as a core concept in gestalt. In chaos theory a similar phenomenon has become known as the 'flipover' effect (Gleick, 1989, p. 29) – the sudden figure/ground shift from one polarity to another. It appears to apply to both process and content – rarely can one polarity remain the same for long without calling its diametrical pole into being. Night follows day, great understanding is linked with great capacity for misunderstanding, great virtue with potential for great vice. Gestaltists such as Beisser (1970), with the articulation of the paradoxical theory of change, used these notions therapeutically in clinical work and we have also used them organisationally. Smuts saw such dynamic interrelatedness as follows:

> Wholes are not closed isolated systems externally: they have their field in which they intermingle and influence each other. The holistic universe is a profoundly reticulated system of interactions and interconnections....
> (Smuts, 1987, p. 333)

Perls *et al.* (1951) also acknowledged the interrelatedness between the individual and society in a most profound way, even though Perls is sometimes interpreted as minimising this interconnectedness. It is clear from the following quotation that this was not the case (but perhaps this was Goodman's particular sensitivity):

> We have been at pains to show that in the organism, ... the social factors are essential... The underlying social nature of the organism and the forming of personality fostering and dependency, communication, imitation and learning, love-choices and companionship, passions of sympathy and antipathy, mutual aid and certain rivalries, – all this is extremely conservative, repressible but ineradicable. And it is meaningless to think of an organism possessing drives which are anti-social in this sense – opposed to his social nature. (p. 333)

The dynamic interrelatedness of all of human life is now a well-established scientific fact. Like quantum physics, chaos theory highlights the importance of *relationships*. In this way, chaos theory has shown us that everything and potentially everybody is related in a kind of dance. Everything is in this sense connected with everything else and any separation is therefore theoretical rather than actual.

> The tension between particles and waves within the wave/particle duality is a tension between being and becoming. Similarly the tension within ourselves between the I and the not-I, between keeping ourselves to ourselves and engaging in more or less intimate relationships is a tension between staying as we are and becoming something new. (Zohar, 1990, p. 114)

Numerous studies show that the relationship is the most significant factor in effective psychotherapy (Norcross, 1986), and gestalt has always acknowledged this. I have elsewhere discussed relationship as a framework for the clinician (Clarkson, 1990), and for those with organisational management, training or development interests (see Chapter 6).

Chaos theory brings another disturbance to our ideas of causality and intervention into systems, for example the possibility that very small interventions or chance occurrences have very large, unpredictable or unknown effects. As Gleick (1989) says,

> Tiny differences in input could quickly become overwhelming differences in output – a phenomenon given the name 'sensitive dependence on initial conditions'. In weather, for example, this translates into what is only half-jokingly known as the Butterfly Effect – the notion that a butterfly stirring the air today in Peking can transform storm systems next month in New York. (p. 8)

However, the greatest difficulties remain, and once we accept that no field exists without an observer, no *me* without the *organisation* around me, no *you* without *us* – how do we effect beneficial changes, who is doing what to whom and why? All the Newtonian notions of causality which so many psychotherapists devotedly apply to human beings (!) may be outdated or even wrong. Taking on board some of these new ideas may require that certain cherished ideas in psychology are relinquished or, at the very best, substantially rethought. The notion that childhood experiences cause adult disturbance is based on notions from a linear, billiard-ball universe, not growing wholes in the process of quantum evolution.

The implications of these notions on organisational work have hardly begun to be felt, but I think some of the most exciting and fruitful opportunities for the future lie precisely in that direction. The detailed working through of this material will be contained in a forthcoming book, at this point called *Gestalt Therapy: A Trinity of Wholes*.

References

Beisser, A. R. (1970). The paradoxical theory of change. In Fagan, J., and Shepherd, I. (eds.), *Gestalt Therapy Now*. Palo Alto, CA: Science and Behavior Books.

Bohm, D. (1983). *Wholeness and the Implicate Order*. London: Ark Paperbacks (first published 1980).

Briggs, J. and Peat, F. D. (1989). *Turbulent Mirror*. New York: Harper & Row (first published 1989).

Capra, F. (1978). *The Turning Point: Science, Society and the Rising Culture*. Toronto: Bantam.

Clarkson, P. (1990). 'A multiplicity of psychotherapeutic relationships', *British Journal of Psychotherapy*, 7(2), 148–63.

Clarkson, P. and MacKewn, J. (1993). *Key Figures in Counselling and Psychotherapy: Fritz Perls*. London: Sage (in press).

Davies, P., interviewed by Macpherson, A. (1992). 'Does this give God His P45?', *The Mail on Sunday*, 26 April, p. 17. London.

Gleick, J. (1989). *Chaos: Making a New Science*. London: Heinemann.

Greenberg, I. A. (ed.) (1975). *Psychodrama: Theory and Therapy*. London: Souvenir Press (first published 1974).

Guerrière, D. (1980). Physis, Sophia, Psyche, pp. 86–134 in J. Sallis & K. Maly (eds.), *Heraclitean Fragments: A Companion Volume to the Heidegger/Fink Seminar on Heraclitus*. Huntsville, AL: University of Alabama Press.

Hawkins, J.M. and Allen, R. (eds.) (1991). *The Oxford Encyclopaedic English Dictionary*. Oxford: Oxford University Press.

Jung, C. G. (1968). Archetypes of the collective unconscious, pp. 3-41 in Sir H. Read, M. Fordham, G. Adler, W. McGuire, (eds.), (R. F. C. Hull, trans.) *The Collected Works of C. G. Jung*, Vol. 9, Part I, (2nd ed.). London: Routledge & Kegan Paul (first published 1954)

Jung, C. G. (1972). *Synchronicity: An Acausal Connecting Principle*. London: Routledge and Kegan Paul (first published 1952).

Mandelbrot, B. B. (1974).*The Fractal Geometry of Nature*. New York: Freeman.

Merleau-Ponty, M. (1970). *Phenomenology of Perception*. London: Routledge & Kegan Paul (first published 1962).

Minkowski, E. (1970). *Lived Time*. Evanston, IL: Northwestern University Press (first published 1933).

Norcross, J. (ed.) (1986). *Handbook of Eclectic Psychotherapy.* New York: Brunner/Mazel.

Perls, F. S. (1969a). *Ego, Hunger and Aggression.* New York: Vintage Books (first published 1947).

Perls, F.S. (1969b). *Gestalt Therapy Verbatim.* Moab, Utah: Real People Press.

Perls, F. S., Hefferline, R. F., and Goodman, P. (1951). *Gestalt Therapy: Excitement and Growth in the Human Personality.* New York: Julian Press.

Runes, D. D. (ed.) (1966). *Dictionary of Philosophy.* Totowa, NJ: Littlefield, Adams & Co.

Schwartz, C., Davidson, G., Seaton, A. and Tebbit, V. (eds.) (1988). *Chambers English Dictionary.* Cambridge: Chambers.

Smuts, J. C. (1987). *Holism and Evolution.* Cape Town, SA: N & S Press (first published 1926).

Wilber, K. (ed.) (1982). *The Holographic Paradigm and Other Paradoxes.* Boulder, CO: Shambhala.

Zohar, D. (1990). *The Quantum Self.* London: Bloomsbury.

Chapter 13
Burn-out

Unhelpful personality patterns of professional helpers

PETRŪSKA CLARKSON

The Problem

The problem is that there is a tendency to burn-out (the depletion of energy levels) in those in the caring professions. This material was developed to show that there is a relationship among scripts, life positions, and Freudenberger's personality types, which is relevant to various predispositions to burn-out in the helping professions. Three typologies, with their associated fairy story characters, were identified as a guide to enhancing understanding for differing personality types' experience of burn-out, not as a characterisation of individuals or a simplistic diagnosis.

Introduction

Since Freudenberger's (1975) pioneering work on burn-out among people in the helping professions, there has been a virtual explosion of interest in, and research about, this particular syndrome. *Webster's Dictionary* (1986 edition) defines the verb burn-out thus: 'To fail, wear out, or become exhausted by reason of excessive demands on energy, strength, or resources'. Maslach (1976) defined it as: 'The loss of concern for the people with whom one is working. . . .(including) physical exhaustion. . . (and) characterised by an emotional exhaustion in which the professional no longer has any positive feelings, sympathy or respect for clients or patients' (p. 18).

There is much concern in the literature (Jaffe *et al*, 1986) and the professions about the prevalence of this burn-out syndrome among caring workers, since it leads to temporary or permanent incapacitation such as exhaustion, loss of creativity and enthusiasm for their work, drug dependence, depression, somatic symptoms and even death, e.g. heart attacks.

Freudenberger's typologies

Freudenberger's classification (1975) includes:

- the dedicated and committed personality type
- the personality type who is overcommitted and whose private life is unsatisfactory
- the authoritarian personality and/or patronising personality type.

In Figure 13.1, these three personality types are related to their respective existential life positions.

Relation to transactional analysis theories

The three life positions Ernst identified in 1971 resemble the three personality types Freudenberger (1975) identified as being sensitive to burn-out. (Administrators or professionals may burn out in a similar way, whichever of these positions they habitually occupy under stress.)

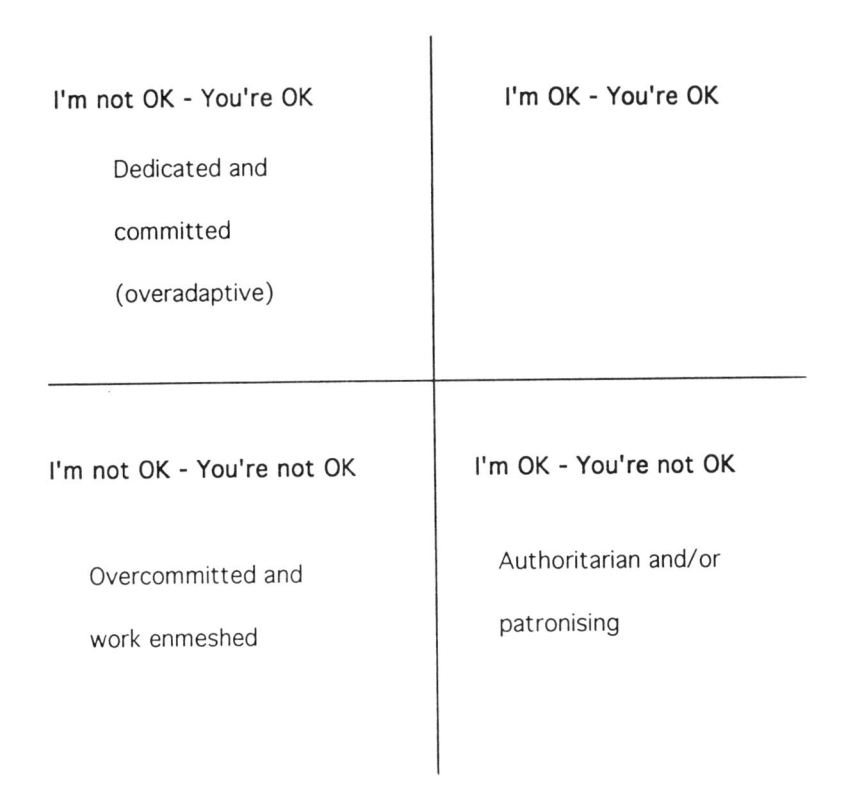

I'm not OK - You're OK Dedicated and committed (overadaptive)	I'm OK - You're OK
I'm not OK - You're not OK Overcommitted and work enmeshed	I'm OK - You're not OK Authoritarian and/or patronising

Figure 13.1 Freudenberger's typology related to Ernst's OK Corral.

Erskine and Zalcman (1979) defined a racket system as 'a self-reinforcing, distorted system of beliefs, thoughts and actions maintained by script-bound individuals. The Racket System has three inter-related and interdependent components: the Script Beliefs and Feelings, the Rackety Displays and the Reinforcing Memories' (p. 53).

Based on the author's clinical experience with large numbers of professional helpers, three distinct racket systems have been identified. Each of these racket systems is associated with one of the not-OK positions, which in turn is related to the Freudenberger typology. Such divisions are obviously based on the identification of general types. This kind of categorisation carries with it both the advantages and disadvantages of stereotyping. It assists professionals in communicating effectively, generalising and teaching from their experience of frequently occurring patterns. However, it is not meant to be used in a reductionistic way which deprives individuals of their existential uniqueness. The fact that this is written with some TA language is a factor of where I first was asked about this material.

Having knowledge about these three generalised racket systems can be helpful for therapists, clients, trainees and workshop participants who are concerned with burn-out phenomena in the helping professions. Psychiatrists, clinical psychologists, social workers, psychotherapists and others may use these formats to identify their own particular predispositions to burn-out in terms of their existential life positions, and to make the necessary changes to their scripts and their lives. They may also be useful also for managers, teachers and supervisors of professional helpers.

The dedicated and committed personality

The dedicated and committed personality is outlined in Table 13.1. Sally is a good example of a dedicated and committed worker. She constantly pushes herself to work hard to meet the increasing demands made upon her. She does not question, nor effectively protest the right of clients or of the institution to make such escalating demands. She is a social worker of deep conviction and cannot say 'no' because of a basic existential belief system which holds that others (and their needs or demands) are worthwhile, while her own needs to protect herself and her psychophysiological resources, and to live a happy, guilt-free life are fundamentally negated. She seeks to earn her OK-ness by her service to others –'I am only OK if I can help you'.

When her efforts meet with less and less success, she works even harder. Despite her decreasing cost-effectiveness, she continues to believe that with longer hours, more dedication, and greater intensity she can make a genuine difference to the flood of demands from the people in the deprived neighbourhood in which she works. Freudenberger (1975) described this as follows:

Table 13.1 A typical dedicated and committed personality type (over-adaptive) racket system

Script beliefs/feelings	Rackety displays	Reinforcing memories
Self: I'm not OK unless I help others I must try harder I am worthless.	Dedicated and committed	**Social level:** rescuer **Psychological level:** victim **Existential level:** persecutor
Others: Are OK (worthwhile), are better /more important than me	**Preferred helping style:** Empathy	
Quality of life: There but for the grace of God go I...	**Reported internal experience:** Worry, then guilt Predominant Child ego state cathexis	(Second-order symbiosis with early caretaker.)
Repressed feelings: Sadness, loss.	**Fantasy:** I will be loved/ appreciated in the end **Fairy story:** Mrs Do-as-you-would-be-done-by, in *The Water-Babies*.	**Helping game:** 'They'll be glad they knew me (in the end)'

What happens is the harder he works, the more frustrated he is, the more bitchy, the more cynical in outlook and behavior – and, of course, the less effective in the very things he so wishes to accomplish. (p. 37)

This vicious cycle compounds Sally's guilt, her feelings of worthlessness, and further depletes her intra-psychic and interpersonal resources. A recurrent motivating dynamic of such personality types is their identification with the victim – the sexually abused girl, the battered wife, the jobless husband caught in a poverty trap, and the person suffering from a physical handicap. By taking care of the hurt child in others, they vicariously seek some solace for the hurt child in themselves. For others, they attempt to be the understanding, generous parent which they never experienced. Out of awareness they have the hope that if they do this long enough and well enough, the grateful client will return these favours. At the very least, the client may demonstrate the love or admiration which they would have wanted from the original parent. The repressed feeling for people like Sally is frequently that of the pain and sadness of loss which is manifested in their inability to establish mutually rewarding, protective, challenging and nourishing relationships with others over the long term.

A fairy story or a story which frequently figures prominently in the childhood of people who are committed and dedicated in this way is Kingsley's *The Water-Babies* (1982). The principal female character, Mrs

Do-as-you-would-be-done-by, represents a position of kindness, consideration and unconditional acceptance of other people, particularly of the small or the defenceless. Tom, the hero, learns through her to be as kind to others as he would like them to be towards him.

The overcommitted and work-enmeshed personality type

The overcommitted and work-enmeshed personality type is outlined in Table 13.2. Freudenberger identified this person as being overcommitted, with an unsatisfactory private life. Work is his or her only source of recognition, and the person's professional and personal lives have merged to the extent that there is no longer any boundary between them. This is the 'I'm not-OK–You're-not-OK' position in the OK Corral. It is easy to become over-involved in a children's home, a free clinic, a crisis intervention unit or a particular ideology such as transactional analysis. Freudenberger (1975) wrote of this personality type:

> The atmosphere and satisfactions can be so seductive that the person finds herself spending even her free time there. But I view this over-involvement as a real danger sign indicating that the worker has given up trying to find meaningful outside activities and relationships (p. 39).

Table 13.2 Typical overcommitted and work-enmeshed personality type racket system

Script beliefs/feelings	Rackety displays	Reinforcing memories
Self: I'm not OK I am lonely and unlovable I am miserable and needy Powerless	Overcommitted, life unsatisfactory.	**Social level:** Victim **Psychological level:** Rescuer **Existential level:** Persecutor
Others: You are not OK	**Preferred helping style:** 'Reality' type therapy.	
Quality of life: Greater love hath no man than to give his life...	**Reported internal experience:** Frustration, then impotence (powerlessness) Alternating Parent and Child ego state cathexis.	(Second-order symbiosis with early caretaker)
Repressed feelings: Despair	**Fantasy:** I/we will survive (It's you and me, babe, against the world.) **Fairy story:** *Thidwick The Big-Hearted Moose*	**Helping game:** Busman's holiday I'm only trying to help you Look how hard I'm trying

John's belief is that service to others is the meaning of life and holds its own ultimate reward. He does not value himself, nor does he deeply believe that his clients or patients can ultimately become independent and autonomous. The task of individuation and separation may be avoided forever. The motivating dynamic of people in the overcommitted and work-enmeshed quadrant is that by sharing the misery and unhappiness and poverty of their clients they promote a feeling of closeness, family and belonging within themselves. Their fantasy is that, by merging their personal and professional selves, they will forever be at home. They will certainly not be lonely. Of course, since the client's capacity and ability to be independent necessarily has to be devalued in this collusive bind, these workers are fundamentally at home with people who do not have many other options for friendship. If the clients were to get well the worker might be deserted and might lose his or her job, status and *raison d'être*.

Due to their over-dedication to their work, these workers or supervisors lack the energy and creativity for a satisfactory private life. They then fail to provide themselves with sufficient satisfaction and reinforcement, and they invest their energy back into work. The repressed feeling is despair, 'the world is a lost cause and all that can be hoped for is to share one another's misery in this vale of tears and oppression'. Nobody can be relied upon to help, least of all people in authority who control the resources (such as management or government). Both professionals and clients are construed as powerless to change the situation.

Thidwick, the Big Hearted Moose, is a character from a children's story who was described as over-kind. He possessed a fine set of antlers and agreed to let a small bug hitch a ride in them. However, the bug then invited a spider to move in and a bird, and although Thidwick found this burdensome he was a good sport and put up with it, as well as with a woodpecker, a squirrel family, a bobcat and other animals who all moved in until they became so heavy that he sank to his knees (Seuss, 1968).

Authoritarian and/or patronising personality type

The authoritarian and/or patronising personality type is outlined in Table 13.3. This is the kind of person 'who so needs to be in control that no one else can do any job as well as he can' (Freudenberger, 1975, p. 39). This person believes that only he or she can do things right, and feels the need to control the budget, the work, the belief systems, even the personal lives if possible, of everybody associated with the institution. They assume that other people are essentially not-OK and lack the intelligence, the education, the capacity, the ego strength to evolve really satisfactory lifestyles for themselves. The current government or psycho-sociological environment are also seen as not-OK. The quality of life would be fine 'If I

Table 13.3 Typical authoritarian and/or patronising personality type racket system

Script beliefs/feelings	Rackety displays	Reinforcing memories
Self: I'm OK I'll get it right I'll save the day	Authoritarian	**Social level:** Persecutor **Psychological level:** Rescuer **Existential level:** Victim
Others: You are not OK, you are inadequate, stupid, incompetent, need controlling.	**Preferred helping style:** Confrontation, potency	
Quality of life: If you can't stand the heat, get out of the kitchen; or, the weakest go to the wall.	**Reported internal experience:** Irritation, self-righteousness Frequent Parent ego state cathexis.	
Repressed feelings: Terror/scared	**Fantasy:** I will be right in the end **Fairy story:** *The Wizard of Oz*	**Helping game:** 'I told you so' N.I.G.Y.S.O.B. Blemish

were in charge of the institution, the country, the world!'

This person's predominant ego state tends to be that of an introjected other, frequently a domineering parent with whom the child made a collusive pact. As a child, this type of person frequently identified with the aggressor, believing that by taking on parental definitions of reality, he could permanently control life and other people. This survival solution, 'Try Hard', sustains a precarious sense of personal OKness.

The fantasy is, 'If the world would listen to me and obey my instructions, we could all be happy. Until then, it is somebody's else's fault'. The repressed feeling is one of terror, the fear is that nobody really knows the answers. No matter how domineering or dominant the parental figure and its pronouncements, this type only succeeds in creating an imposing Wizard of Oz behind which shelters a rather scared and inadequate person. 'The Wizard turns out to be a little, old, bald-headed man who admits to being a fraud' (Baum, 1982, p. 37).

Summary

Observation of several hundred members of helping professions such as physicians, psychologists, social workers, nurses, psychiatrists and clinical psychologists, suggests that there are three frequently occurring and characteristic types of script-bound personality which are predisposed to burn-out as described above. Such observation can lead to effective prevention of burn-out by enhancing awareness of one's own particular predisposition so as to take remedial and preventative action. Supervisors and managers too can use such observation to make interventions that will prevent burn-out.

A Case Study

Returning to the example of Sally, the social worker typical of a dedicated and committed personality type worker, it was being transferred to a different area team with a more experienced and observant supervisor that helped prevent her 'burning out'. Her supervisor, aware of the dangers of Sally working from a deficit position (I'm not OK–You're OK) and of needing to be loved by clients, soon intervened in Sally's already increasing client-load by sharing her concern and recommending a more balanced ratio of client-contact time to administrative time. She further advised an earlier holiday than Sally had intended and suggested that a weekly massage would be a good start in building her stroke economy. On seeing how she was perpetuating a cycle of worthlessness through operating from her characteristic over-adaptive racket system, Sally was willing to contract for these changes with her supervisor in order to break the cycle.

The I'm OK–You're OK Position

Since the racket system is characteristic of script-bound individuals, it is assumed that script-free individuals do not have a characteristic racket system susceptible to burn-out, though they will, of course, have a place; namely, the I'm OK–You're OK position. Script-free individuals may have predispositions towards these three particular types of manifestation, but have made the necessary re-decisions, integrations and growth to maturity which would render full-scale activation of any of these racket systems unlikely. Because such individuals are spontaneous, aware, and proactive in the work situation from moment to moment, their behaviour may at times resemble that of any of the three racket systems described because they are not exempt from pain, frustration or doubt. Individuals who are mostly in Integrated Adult mode and who are free from the more severe stringencies of their scripts, and who are living in concert with the changing demands of the moment-by-moment existential encounter, cannot be fitted into a system. Autonomy, spontaneity and intimacy cannot be mapped; they can only be lived.

The effective management and resolution of these non-productive or destructive (third-degree) script decisions as they are presented in terms of the currently fashionable concepts of burn-out, are no different from those which are used for any other kind of symptomatology in transactional analysis.

Summary

For Freud, the two most important things in life were to love and to work. Discovering and celebrating the fluctuating rhythm between these two may take a lifetime.

References

Baum, F. L. (1982). *The Wizard of Oz*. Harmondsworth: Puffin (first published in 1900).

Ernst, Jr., F. H. (1971). 'The OK Corral: The grid for get-on-with', *Transactional Analysis Journal*, 1(4), 33–42.

Erskine, R. G. and Zalcman, M. J. (1979). 'The racket system', *Transactional Analysis Journal*, 9(1), 51–9.

Freudenberger, H. J. (1975). 'The staff burn-out syndrome in alternative institutions', *Psychotherapy: Theory, Research and Practice*, 12(1), 35–45.

Jaffe, D.T., Scott, C.D. and Orioli, E.M. (1986). 'Stress management: programs and prospects', *American Journal of Health Promotion*, 1, 29–37.

Kingsley, C. (1982). *The Water-Babies*. London: Hodder & Stoughton (first published in 1863).

Maslach, C. (1976). 'Burned-out', *Human Behaviour*, 5(9), 16–22.

Seuss, Dr (1968). *Thidwick the Big-Hearted Moose*. London: Collins.

Index

absenteeism, 13
absorption, as blocking mechanism, 21
Achilles syndrome, *see* pseudocompetent executives
action-learning programmes, 64
action phase of cycles, 18, 19
adapted group imago, 94-95
adjourning stage, group development, 102
alcoholism, 13
anticipation, as blocking mechanism, 21
anxiety, groups, 92
attitudes, useful, 109, 114-116
authenticity, personal relationships, 52
authoritarian personality type, 145-146
autocracies, 91
autonomy, illusion of, 32
avoidance, as blocking mechanism, 21
awareness continuum, 131-132
awareness stage of cycles, 18, 19

Berne, Eric, 85, 86, 87, 88-89, 104
big bang, 134
blocks to cycles, 21-22
　dysfunctional, 23
Bohm, D., 130
Bohr, Niels, 110
Boydell, T., 65
BP, 83
Bragg, Wiliam (Sir), 110
Branson, Richard, 53
breakdown, *see* distress
Briggs, J., 111, 112, 130, 134
British Petroleum (BP), 83
bureaucracy
　and bystanding, 125
　transpersonal relationships, lack of, 53
burn-out, 140-148
　organisationally precipitated difficulties, 12
　transpersonal relationships, lack of, 53
butterfly effect, 113, 137
bystanders, 117, 121-125

career consultancy, 14, 49
causality, end of, 115-116
caution, 4
Chambers, I., 114
chaos theory, 53
　flipover effect, 136
　holism, 130
　metaphor, 111-112
　relationships, importance of, 137
child development theories, 11
clarified group imago, 101-102
Clarkson, Petrūska, *x, xv,* 5, 10, 13, 14, 24, 25, 34, 43, 55, 58, 59, 60, 75, 84, 116, 117, 118, 119, 125, 130, 137, 138
coaching, 58
collective contribution to planet, 8, 12-13
collective evolution, 8, 12-13
committed personality type, 138, 142-145, 147
communication
　computer technologists, 57-58
　as core competency, 3
competence, 78
　and pseudocompetence, 79, 80

149

completion phase of cycles, 18
comprehension, 3
computer technologists, 57-58
conduct, 4
conflict, 37-38, 41
confluence, as blocking mechanism, 22
confusion, 36-37, 41
connection, 3
constructive behaviours, group development
   forming stage, 93
   mourning stage, 104
   norming stage, 99
   performing stage, 100
   storming stage, 96
consultants
   core competencies, 1-5
   types, 2
contact phase of cycles, 18, 19
contract, as core competency, 2-3
Cottone, R. R., 111
counselling services, 56-57, 58-59
   developmental relationships, 50
   and personal development, differences between, 65-67
   and professional development, boundaries between, 70-74
   trend towards, 44-45
countertransference
   group development, 92
   prioritising organisational interventions, 41
   unfinished relationships, 47
cover-ups, pseudocompetency, 81
creativity, 28
   and conflict, 38
   and stability, 112
   in working alliances, 49
credit, 4
current world conditions, 107-108
cycle of human experience, 15-17
   awareness of, 115, 131-135
   health and disease, 17
   interruptions to, 21-23
   phases, 17-18

danger, 35-36, 41
dedicated personality type, 142-144, 147
deflection, as blocking mechanism, 21, 22
deficit, 39, 41

democracies, 91
de-personalising, 73
destructive behaviours, group development
   forming stage, 93
   mourning stage, 104
   norming stage, 99
   performing stage, 100
   storming stage, 96
destructive change, 31
developmental relationships, 44, 45, 49-51, 54
developmental stages in groups
   forming stage of groups, 89, 90, 92
   mourning stage of groups, 101, 102
   norming stage of groups, 97, 98
   performing stage of groups, 98, 101
   storming stage of groups, 94, 97
developmental stressors, *see* eustress
dialogic communication, 3
differential outcomes of organisational change, 26-27
   destructive change, 31
   fake change, 32
   impossible change, 30-31
   no change, 29-30
   real change, 27-29
differential group imago, 100
disease in human cycles, 17
disillusionment, 30-31
disintegrating organisations, 31
distress, 8, 10, 11-12, 13, 28
dynamic interrelatedness, 135-138

Eco, Umberto, 113
education, 58
egotism, as blocking mechanism, 22
empowerment
   and bystanders, 122
   problems, 54
enantiodromia, 136
ending phase of cycles, 18
Erhard, Werner, 61
Ernst, Jr., F. H., 141
Erskine, R. G., 142
Est programme, 61
Esterson, A., 115
eustress, 8, 10, 12, 13, 28
evolutionary change, 26, 27
expectation management, 70
experience, cycle of, 15-17

# Index

health and disease, 17
    interruptions to, 21-23
    phases, 17-18
facilitative behaviours, 109, 117-118
facility, paradoxical, 115-116
fake change, 32
fantasy projection, as blocking mechanism, 21
flipover effect, 136
forming stage, group development, 89-93
Foucault's pendulum, 113-114
fractals, 111-113, 119, 131
Frankl, V., 124-125
Freudenberger, H. J., 140, 141-147
future fitness, 107

Gaia hypothesis (Lovelock), 53
Geldof, Bob, 53
generalising, 73
gestalt, 126-128
    change, cycle of, 131-135
    dynamic interrelatedness, 135-138
    holism, 128-131
    transpersonal relationships, 53
Gleick, J., 111, 137
gossip, 83
group development, 85, 87-88
    forming stage, 89-93
    mourning stage, 101-104
    norming stage, 97-98
    performing stage, 98-101
    storming stage, 94-97
group dynamics, 17, 119
group imago, 85, 87, 88-89
    adapted, 94-95
    clarified, 101-102
    differentiated, 100
    operative, 97-98
    provisional, 89-90
    secondarily adjusted, 98-99
groups, 85-87
    relationships in, 116-117
    self-creating, 119
groupwork, development of, 14
growth stressors, see eustress
Gurowitz, E. M., 91

Harrison, R., 56
Hawthorne studies, 11, 43
healthy systems, cycles in, 17

Heisenberg, W., 111
Heraclitus, 115, 128-129, 132-133, 136
holism, 128-131
homeostasis, 8, 9-10
honesty, in personal relationships, 51, 52
human relationships, 43-46
    counselling and consulting, implications for, 53-54
    developmental, 49-51
    gestalt, 137
    metaphor, 111
    personal, 51-52
    transpersonal, 52-53
    unfinished, 46-48
    working alliances, 48-49
humour, 118

Icarus, 31
imago, group see group imago
impossible change, 30-31
impressions, good, 80-81
imputed leadership, 113
incompetence, 78
    and pseudocompetence, 79
interpretation, 71
interrelatedness, dynamic, 135-138
interruptions to cycles, 17
    as dysfunctional blocks, 23
    usefulness as coping mechanisms, 21-22
introjection, as blocking mechanism, 21, 22
intuition, 117

Kubler-Ross, E., 102-103

Lacoursiere, R., 85, 87-88, 104
Laing, R. D., 115
laughter, 118
leadership
    group development
        forming stage, 90-93
        mourning stage, 102-104
        norming stage, 98
        performing stage, 101
        storming stage, 95-97
    imputed, 113
    personal development and professional development groups, 62-64, 68-70

personal development and therapy groups, 66
and transpersonal relationships, 53
learning process, professional and personal development, 63, 64-65
Lewin, 135
light metaphor, 110-111
Lincoln, Abraham, 118
listening, 3
long-range planning, 82-83

management consultants, 34-42
management training programmes, 61
Mandelbrot, B. B., 111, 131
mandorla 57
marital problems of staff, 13
Maslach, C., 140
Medea, 31
mentoring
  developmental relationships, 50, 51
  professional development, 58
merging, as blocking mechanism, 22
Merleau-Ponty, M., 127
metanoia
  fake change, 32
  gestalt 134
  openness to, 115
metanoia Training Institute, ix, 128
metaphors
  interventions, 72-73
  for understanding, 109-114
Minkowski, E., 127
mission statements, 12
  transpersonal relationships, 52
mobilisation phase of cycles, 18, 19
modelling, 71-72
modernism, 113-114
motivation in human relationships, 44, 45
Mould, G., 83, 108, 114
mourning stage, group development, 101-104

necessary skills, 109, 116-117
no change, 29-30
non-bystanding, 117
normalising, 71, 73
norming stage, group development, 97-98
numbness, as blocking mechanism, 21

Odysseus, 28-29
Oedipus, 32
operative group imago, 97-98
opposites, dynamic interrelatedness, 135-136
organisational consulting, 1-6
organisationally precipitated difficulties, 8, 11-12
over-adaptive personality type, 143
overcommitted personality type, 144-146

paradoxical facility, 115-116
patronising personality type, 145-146
Pavlov's dogs, 77, 108
Peat, F. D., 112, 130, 134
performing stage, group development, 98-101
Perls, F. S., 127
  change, cycle of, 132, 133-134
  dynamic interrelatedness, 136-137
  holism, 129, 130, 131
permissions in natural cycles, 19, 20
personal development, 56-58, 61-62
  leader's role, 62-64, 68
  and professional development, differences and boundaries between, 62-65, 68-70
  and therapy, differences between, 65-67
personal difficulties, 8, 11
personal disintegration, 8, 11
personal excellence, 8, 12
personal relationships, 44, 45, 51-52, 54
persuasion, 3
Physis, 132, 136
postmodernism, 113-114
preparation phase of cycles, 18
prescriptive interventions, 74
Pribram, 130-131
prioritising organisational interventions, 34-35, 42
  diagnostic framework, 35-41
production lines, 53
professional development, 56-58
  and counselling, boundaries between, 70-74
  leader's role, 62-64, 68
  and personal development, differences and boundaries between, 62-65, 68-69

Index

professionalisation, 79
progress, 29-30
projected relationships, *see* unfinished relationships
projection, as blocking mechanism, 22
provisional group imago, 89-90
pseudocompetency, 51, 76-82, 116
    gossip, 83
    long-range planning, 82-83
    organisational rules, changing, 83-84
psychodrama, 135
psychotherapy, 56-57, 58-61
    and personal development, differences between, 65-67
    and professional development, boundaries between, 70-74

quantum field theory, 134
quantum group dynamics, 119
quantum physics
    connectivity, 53
    metaphor, 110-111

racket systems, 143-146, 147-148
reactive organisations, 30
real change, 27-29
redundancy, 15
    fear of, 36
redundancy counselling, 15
    cycle of human experience, 15-17
        health and disease, 17
        interruptions to, 21-23
        phases, 17-18
        therapeutic process, 18-19
    unblocking the client, 23-25
    unfinished business concept, 19-20
relocations, 13
representative samples, 131
restructuring, 13
retroflection, as blocking mechanism, 21-22
revolutionary change, 26, 27
rhetoric, 3
Roddick, Anita, 53

satisfaction phase of cycles, 18, 19
secondarily adjusted group imago, 98-99
self-actualisation, 8, 12
self-consciousness, as blocking mechanism, 22

self-creating groups, 119
self-criticism, as blocking mechanism, 21-22
self-disclosure, 71, 72
Selye, Hans, 9-10, 12, 28
sensation phase of cycles, 18, 19
shame, 80, 81
Sisyphus, 30
skilled facilitators, 67
skills for the future, 109, 116-117
Smuts, Jan, 130, 133, 136
spontaneity, 71, 72
stability, 112
storming stage, group development, 94-97
stress, 8, 9-10, 13
    counselling, 7-14
    and no change, 29
    and real change, 28
structural interventions, 72, 74
structure
    group, 92
    professional and personal development, 63, 65
supervision, 58
synchronicity, 135
systemic destruction 8, 12

talking, 3
therapeutic aspects
    of counselling, 18-19
    of developmental relationships, 50
time structures, and group development, 92
timing of actions, 4
Tittmarr, H. G., 8
training, 65
    professional development, 58
transactional analysis, 86, 87
transferential relationships *see* unfinished relationships
transpersonal relationships, 44, 45, 52-53, 54
trust, in personal relationships, 51, 52
Tuckman, B. W., 85, 87, 88, 104
    forming stage of groups, 90
    norming stage of groups, 97
    performing stage of groups, 99
    storming stage of groups, 94

unblocking the client, 23-25

uncertainty principle (Heisenberg), 111
understanding, metaphors for, 109-114
unfinished business concept, 19-20
unfinished relationships, 44, 45-48, 54
    developmental relationships, contrasts between, 50
unlearning, 117-118

void, 134-135
volume control, 4

wholeness, 112-113
Wilber, K., 131
withdrawal
    by consultant, 4
    cycle phase, 18, 19
    group development phase, 102
Worden, J. W., 102
work, need to, 77-78
work-enmeshed personality type, 144-145
working alliances, 44, 45, 48-49, 54
writing, 3

Zalcman, M. J., 142
Zaphiropoulos, Renn, 47
Zinker, J., 60
Zohar, D., 134, 137